Blessi King of the Universe

Blessing the King of the Universe

Transforming Your Life
Through the Practice
of Biblical Praise

IRENE LIPSON

Lederer Books
a division of
Messianic Jewish Publishers

Unless otherwise indicated, Scripture quotations are taken from, and follow the format of, the *Complete Jewish Bible*, Copyright © 1998 by David H. Stern, published by Jewish New Testament Publications, Inc. Used by permission.

Printed in the United States of America

09 08 07 06 05 04   6 5 4 3 2 1
ISBN 1-880226-79-0

Library of Congress Control Number: 2004105484

Lederer Books
a division of
Messianic Jewish Publishers
6204 Park Heights Ave.
Baltimore, Maryland 21215
(410) 358-6471

Distributed by
Messianic Jewish Resources International
Individual and Trade order line: (800) 410-7367
E-mail: lederer@messianicjewish.net
Website: www.messianicjewish.net

Dedicated to the memory of my late husband, Eric Lipson

זכר צדיק לברכה

Zecher Tzaddik Liv'rachah

The memory of the righteous shall be for a blessing (Proverbs 10:7).

Contents

Foreword

To understand the value of this book, it might be best to think of it as a bridge, a window, and a friend.

In this work, Irene Lipson shares from her life of insights enriched by her marriage to Eric Peter Lipson, whose memory is a blessing. In the 1980s, I had the privilege of meeting Eric and of co-officiating with him in a wedding, in England. Even then, he was well on in years, cultured, thoroughly educated in Jewish life, personifying holiness expressing itself in conspicuous human decency and lovingkindness. Eric came to faith in Yeshua in England, in the aftermath of World War II. His spiritual mentor, Jakob Jocz, was himself a bridge between the vanished world of the Eastern European and the Jewish and Christian communities of England, and later North America, and through his writings, the rest of the world. As Jocz was a bridge to his world for Eric, Eric was bridge to his world and Jacob's for Irene. Through this book, Irene is a bridge from their world—a world of European Hebrew Christianity enhanced by a deeper than usual knowledge and love of Jewish life—to the rest of us.

Irene, and her book, are bridges to Jewish life for those eager to have their own spiritual lives refreshed from the springs of Judaism. The chief value of this book is in how it makes Jewish life and sensibilities accessible to those who want to bridge the world of Jewish life and the world of belief in Yeshua, the Messiah of Israel and the nations. And, as Irene and Eric were bridges between British Hebrew Christianity and Messianic Judaism, with its richer immersion in Jewish community and religious life, so this book is a living bridge between what was and what is coming to be.

Mrs. Lipson accomplishes her aims through employing *b'rakhot*, Jewish blessings, as a window into Jewish religious life and the life of Yeshua and the Apostles. Beyond telling us what *b'rakhot* are, she shows what they mean for the individual and the congregation, in the context of ordinary days and holy occasions. She demonstrates how they played a key role in the life of Yeshua and the Apostles, and how they might play an important part in our lives as well. Each chapter ends with a prayer from Irene, and a *b'rakhah* of her own devising. In this, each chapter provides a model for the reader to imitate in enriching their own spiritual life.

Irene freely admits that the purpose of her book is "devotional," that is, to enhance personal spirituality and religious practice. She succeeds in this endeavor quite well. Christian readers will especially find this book valuable, as it provides a clear window into Jewish life, the New Testament, and a more rewarding spiritual life for each reader.

Finally, this book is a friend—the kind of friend Eric Lipson was, and Irene continues to be. As they are intelligent, articulate friends, well-versed in Jewish life and deeply committed to the kingdom of God's Messiah, Yeshua, so this book is an educational, intelligent, articulate friend. *Blessing the King of the Universe* not only presents priceless information from thousands of years of Jewish life, but also provides a model of integration for those seeking to enhance their own devotional life from a Jewish perspective.

Readers will benefit from Irene Lipson's wide reading and robust appreciation of creation. They will also gain from her appreciation of the redemption and hope God has given us, as well as her deep spiritual sensitivity. You will find yourself saying as I did, "I would love to have this woman pray for me," because above all else, this book breathes the atmosphere of Irene's deep relationship, not only with the people of Israel, but even more so, with the God of Israel. She is a good friend to have. And so is this book.

You are in for a treat. Enjoy!

—Rabbi Stuart Dauermann, Ph.D.
Ahavat Zion Messianic Synagogue, Beverly Hills, California

Introduction—Blessing God, a Privilege and a Delight!

The practice of saying a blessing—or "making" a ברכה (b'rakhah—blessing)—has been, for me, one of the most delightful aspects of Jewish life. I came from a non-Jewish background and found, or was found by, Yeshua (Jesus) within the Church. Then I met Eric Lipson, a new Jewish believer in Messiah. He was exploring how to reconcile his new faith with his Jewishness. In those days, most Hebrew Christians (as they were then called) were strongly encouraged to assimilate into churches and maintain a non-Jewish lifestyle. However, Eric was never afraid to be different. He loved his Jewish culture and would not abandon it. He and his father and grandfather had been synagogue leaders. He saw Yeshua as the fulfillment of Judaism, not its destruction.

I had been working with a missionary society in Egypt. There, Jewish believers, largely French-speaking, were expected to worship using the English *Book of Common Prayer,* written in the seventeenth century! Together, Eric and I set off on the adventure of maintaining a Jewish lifestyle in Messiah Yeshua. To today's Messianic Jews, our efforts may seem insignificant and ineffective. Back then there was no Messianic Jewish community with which to identify—and community, of course, is crucial to Judaism. It is the fate of pioneers to experiment and to make mistakes. We were no exception. However, we did discover treasures. Among those riches were the *b'rakhot* (blessings). We derived great joy in making *b'rakhot* in our new life in Messiah.

I have written this book to share the delight of those treasures. Rather than a theological exposition, it is designed as a series of short meditations on a selection of the *b'rakhot.* Studying these *b'rakhot* can bring a new dimension to your devotional life and fresh challenges to your daily walk in the Messiah. Let me now introduce you to the background of the *b'rakhot.*

The Talmud

The Talmud is a vast, complex anthology of Jewish law and the traditions that accumulated around that law over the course of several hundred years. These traditions themselves became accepted as law. The kernel of what we now have in written form was passed down orally from generation to generation through the centuries. According to Jewish tradition, Moses received the verbal component on Sinai. It then passed down the generations. Eventually it was committed to writing around the year 200 C.E. (the common era), possibly to ensure its preservation in a time of national catastrophe. Thus, the Mishnah came into being.

After 70 C.E. and the destruction of the Temple by Rome, something was needed to replace the Temple as the cohesive force in Judaism. The Mishnah became the focus of rabbinical study and discussion in synagogue life. In time, the rabbis collected these discussions, known as the Gemara. There were two such collections: the *Talmud Yerushalami* (the Jerusalem Talmud) and the *Talmud Bavli* (the Babylonian Talmud). The word *Talmud* derives from the same root as the Hebrew word for disciple (*talmid*). Mishnah and Gemara together form the Talmud. A typical page of the more familiar Babylonian Talmud has the Mishnah passage (in Hebrew) in the center, with the various commentaries and discussions (usually in Aramaic) arranged round it. This work was completed about the year 500 C.E.

That was not the end of the matter. The eleventh-century theologian Rashi wrote a commentary on the Talmud, and his commentary became the subject of further comment and discussion. These collected comments are known as *Tosefta*. The process of commenting on commentaries continues to this day.

Yeshua knew the verbal traditions as well as the written *Tanakh* (Hebrew Scriptures, or "Older" Testament). He treated his heritage with respect, and so we must do the same.

Tractate *B'rakhot*

B'rakhot is the first of the sixty-three tractates (volumes) of the Talmud. It contains the daily prayers that a Jewish person ought to offer, either in private or in the congregation, as well as the blessings that one should utter on various occasions. There are nine chapters in this tractate. The first three are about the saying of the *Sh'ma*, beginning, "Hear, O Israel, the Lord our God, the Lord is One" (Deut. 6:4). The next two deal with prayer in general. The last four chapters concern blessings that one may recite on various occasions. In this last section, we find blessings pertaining to the partaking of food as well as discussions between the two schools of Shammai and Hillel (first-century C.E. teachers) concerning those blessings. Here, too, are blessings relating to events that cause awe, joy, or grief.

Maimonides, the great twelfth-century theologian and philosopher, had an explanation for why tractate *B'rakhot* is the first in the Talmud. He suggested that to be in good health one must eat and that before eating one must recite the appropriate *b'rakhah*. It follows, therefore, that the subject of the *b'rakhot* needs to precede all else.

In any case, the *b'rakhot* are at the heart of Judaism. The rabbis have taught that one should not undertake anything of worth without first making the appropriate blessing. The injunction applies to everything, from the reciting of the *Sh'ma* to the eating of food.

There is a *b'rakhah* for almost every conceivable situation, including regular times of prayer and before and after the eating of a meal. Specific *b'rakhot* were written for different kinds of food and fragrances, occasions, and experiences. One should regard everything as an opportunity to bless the Lord.

The Beginning of the *B'rakhot*

Tradition has it that the *b'rakhot* were formulated during the time of Ezra, after the return from Exile. However, the custom of blessing the Lord goes back much further than that. The suggestion has been made that some *Tehillim* (Psalms)—for example, Psalms 136, 147, and 148— were the basis for the *b'rakhot*. Rabbi Binyamin Forst, speaking of *b'rakhot* associated with food, has said that although most are rabbinical in origin, the *birkat ha'mazon* (grace after meals) is biblical (Forst 38). The text of most of the *b'rakhot* was established around the year 350 B.C.E. (before the common era) by the men of the "Great Assembly" (Forst 35).

In time, the custom became established that "every manifestation of divine protection and help became an opportunity for the pious Israelite to offer up thanksgiving in the usual form of a benediction" ("Benedictions"). Eventually opportunity became regulation. The Talmud states that Rabbi Meir, a second-century scholar, declared it to be the duty of everyone to say a hundred *b'rakhot* each day (*Menahot* 43b).

In Rabbi Meir's day, there was a dispute about the form of *b'rakhot*. Could one offer spontaneous thanks, or must one adhere to the set phrasing (*Ber.* 40b)? The fear that the ignorant might blaspheme unwittingly was always present. It was safer to have a rigidly prescribed wording. The Steinsaltz Talmud notes: "It is forbidden to alter the wording of the prayers and blessings as fixed by the Sages." It seems, however, that a minor deviation is not regarded too seriously as long as the original meaning is retained (225). The form of words used for obligatory *b'rakhot* is usually different from that used for spontaneous ones.

Obligatory *b'rakhot* must open with the full "preamble." Others may shorten this. For instance: "Blessed art thou, the true judge."

Classes of *B'rakhot*

The blessings belong to different categories. The usual division is this: (1) blessings of enjoyment; (2) blessings over the privilege of performing a *mitzvah* (religious duty); (3) blessings of thanksgiving and praise. The third category may include the occasions of meeting certain people, experiencing unusual events, and seeing beautiful phenomena in nature. If one is visiting a place with special memories, happy or tragic, there will be an appropriate blessing for the occasion. Indeed, one can assume that there is a *b'rakhah* for every eventuality. In the musical *Fiddler on the Roof,* when the rabbi was asked, "Is there a blessing for a sewing machine?" his answer was categorical: "There's a blessing for everything."

The principle is that everything one enjoys requires a *b'rakhah* (*Ber.* 35a). To withhold that response to God's goodness is to rob him (*Ber.* 35b). However, the duty is more a delight than a burden. There is joy in competing to see who can be the first to see the sea, in catching sight of a rainbow, in tasting the first of the new season's fruit. For all these, and for many other experiences, there is an appropriate *b'rakhah.*

The Structure of a *B'rakhah*

Every *b'rakhah* begins with the words *"Barukh atah Adonai Eloheynu Melekh ha'olam"* ("Blessed are you, O Lord our God, King of the universe"). We bless the Lord, mentioning his name and his kingship. As it states in Deuteronomy 32:3, "I will proclaim the name of ADONAI. Come, declare the greatness of our God!" After that formula come words appropriate to the occasion. Sometimes, in the case of blessings not laid down by the sages, we may omit the words "O Lord our God, King of the universe" (Friedlander 444).

Significantly, every *b'rakhah* begins in the second person, addressing God by name and title: "Blessed are *you,* O Lord our God." Having thus acknowledged not only who he is but also our relationship to him, we then move into the third person, describing his will and his commands. It is as if we begin by perceiving his immediate, personal presence. We then move on to describing his essence, at which point we become conscious of his "otherness." The God with whom we are intimately related is yet far beyond our comprehension (Forst 29).

Why the B'rakhot?

"Our sages regarded it as their duty not only to call us from the turmoil of life to a gathering to God, but to approach us *in life itself*, in order to make vivid for us the thought of God in life, and to help us towards an active life in the service of God. They fulfilled this task by means of the *b'rakhot* which they offered us" (Hirsch 521). Thus the pronouncing of a *b'rakhah* is also an act of submission, of dedication. Hirsch further stated,

> In all forms of the berachoth, you approach God, and say to Him: I wish to dedicate myself to Your service . . . You, Who are omnipresent . . . Who is our God; the same One Who, being omnipresent, surrounds, impregnates, and rules our whole life invisibly as the Master of all that time produces; to Whom every work, mission, gift, institution, appointment, being, creature, phenomenon, enjoyment, duty and event in our life belongs. (522)

The pleasure is not all one-sided. Louis Jacobs, an eminent mid-twentieth-century English rabbi, attributed to Isaac Bashevis Singer, the Yiddish novelist, the story of a *Hasid* (a member of a Jewish sect that worships God with exuberance and joy). This *Hasid* used to say, "It is good to be a Jew."

> What greater pleasure can there be than being a Jew? . . . If a person were to offer me all the gold in the world . . . on condition that I skip one blessing, I would laugh in his face. These are vanity, trifles, not worth an empty egg-shell. But when I recite the blessing: "By whose word all things exist," I feel renewed strength in my very bones. Just think of it: "Blessed art Thou, O Lord our God, King of the Universe, by Whose word all things exist." All things, all! The heavens, the earth, I, you. . . . All were created by Him, the Creator, and to us He gave the power to praise Him. Is this not sufficient earthly pleasure? (Jacobs, *Principles* 151)

At times, one may make a *b'rakhah* at a time, not of joy, but of sorrow. There can be great peace in the realization that one is not alone in the situation. God is in control of his created universe; one's destiny is safe in his hands. "It is possible to experience a deep and abiding *simchah* [joy] in the knowledge that man is not alone and adrift" (Forst 24).

My Prayer for You

Study should not be an end in itself; it should lead to worship. It is my hope, therefore, that this book will be used not only as study material but also as a devotional aid. My prayer is that the practice of making a *b'rakhah* may draw us back to an attitude of awe and reverence. That should be the essence of our relationship with the God of our fathers (Forst 26). We need the constant reminder that our lives are to be sanctified to a holy God (Forst 24).

Chapter 1

Pray As Yeshua Did

Asked to fill in a form including a little box marked "religion," Yeshua would unhesitatingly have checked the box marked "Jewish." He was not a Christian. "Christian" was the name given to his early followers after Gentiles started believing in large numbers (Acts 11:26). Yeshua was born, lived, and died a devout, practicing Jew. This was the milieu into which God chose to send his Son, the Messiah of Israel and the Savior of the world.

Not all of Yeshua's contemporaries were devout or practicing, just as not all Jewish people today are religious. Among the most devout back then were the Pharisees. Compared to other groups of Yeshua's day, such as the Sadducees and the Essenes, Messiah fit more closely with the Pharisees than with any other group.

The Pharisees have had some bad press. Not all of them were hypocrites. Many, in fact, were truly God-fearing individuals. Nicodemus the Pharisee came to Yeshua seeking truth, subsequently following him when it was dangerous to do so (John 3:1–2; 19:38–40). Gamaliel the Pharisee counseled the Sanhedrin,

> Men of Isra'el, take care what you do to these people . . . my advice to you is not to interfere with these people, but to leave them alone. For if this idea or this movement has a human origin, it will collapse. But if it is from God, you will not be able to stop them; you might even find yourselves fighting God! (Acts 5:35, 38–39)

The Roots of Tradition

Judaism is a religion that has grown and developed through the centuries. While some claim that it has not fundamentally changed, it has certainly reacted to the pressures put upon it by the professing Church over time. The reason for such stability lies in one important word— "tradition." Tradition has it that on Sinai God gave Moses a body of oral directions that was not put into writing. Moses handed that oral law on to Joshua. From him it passed to the elders, then to the prophets, then to the men of the Great Synagogue. They followed Ezra after the return from the Babylonian captivity. The Judaism we know today developed from that beginning (*Av.* 1:1). This material, known today as Mishnah, was not written down until around the year 200 C.E., when it was edited by Rabbi *Yehudah HaNasi* (Judah the Prince). In the following centuries, commentary and yet more commentary was added until the Talmud was completed around 500 C.E. In Yeshua's day, there was no written Mishnah, no Talmud, as the Jewish people have today. However, Yeshua would have been familiar with its basic material in its oral form. Consider the good impression he made on the rabbis during his boyhood visit to the Temple (Luke 2:46–47). This would not have been possible if he was not well-versed in the traditions.

Yeshua and Tradition

It is a mistake to say that Yeshua dismissed all Jewish traditions. He directed his criticism at two groups of people: (1) those who placed tradition on a par with—or even above—the written Scriptures (Matt. 15:6; Mark 7:8); and (2) those who distorted and misused tradition. An example of the latter type of criticism is his condemnation of those who wore oversized *tefillin* (phylacteries) for reasons of pride (Matt. 23:5). *Tefillin* are small boxes, containing passages of Scripture, which are worn on the forehead and upper arm during prayers. The custom is a response to Deuteronomy 6:8: "Tie them on your hand as a sign, put them at the front of a headband around your forehead."

Yeshua was at home within in Judaism at its best. His sayings (which sometimes echo those of other great rabbis), his formulation of the "Lord's Prayer" (Matt. 6:9–13), and his celebration of the Passover *seder* (celebration meal)—all these were culturally and religiously familiar to the people among whom he lived.

Yeshua and the *B'rakhot*

As we look at the religious world in which Yeshua lived, we will come to understand the meaning behind many of his words and actions. This includes the role of *b'rakhot* in his life. Central to Judaism now and as it has been through the ages is the idea of blessing God.

The first tractate of the Talmud is *B'rakhot*. This is the prayer directory of religious Jewish people. It deals with the three required elements of the prayer life: (1) the saying of the *Sh'ma*; (2) the whole prayer life; (3) the *b'rakhot* that one may recite on various occasions. The *b'rakhot* give to Judaism its characteristic stamp—awe of the one, true God; the development of a God-centered life; the sanctifying of the ordinary experiences of life.

We can be quite sure that Yeshua grew up learning many *b'rakhot*. He learned to bless God in the breaking of bread and the drinking of wine. He blessed the God of might in the storm, the God of faithfulness on seeing a rainbow, and the God of life in the presence of death. Jewish people have done so through the ages—and still do today. Yeshua was no different.

Surely Yeshua was making a *b'rakhah* when responding to the reports of the seventy *talmidim* (disciples):

> He was filled with joy by the *Ruach HaKodesh* [Holy Spirit] and said, "Father, Lord of heaven and earth, I thank [bless] you because you concealed these things from the sophisticated and educated, yet revealed them to ordinary people. Yes, Father, I thank [bless] you that it pleased you to do this." (Luke 10:21)

When he fed the five thousand, "he took the five loaves and the two fish and, looking up toward heaven, made a *b'rakhah*" (Matt. 14:19). The words would have been "Blessed are you, O Lord our God, King of the universe, who brings forth bread from the earth."

People responded to his miracles in the familiar Jewish way. When the crowds witnessed the healing of the paralytic, "they were awestruck and said a *b'rakhah* to God the Giver of such authority to human beings" (Matt. 9:8). As they watched his multiple healings, they were amazed and "they said a *b'rakhah* to the God of Isra'el" (Matt. 15:31).

As we look at this aspect of Yeshua's life, we can learn new ways of drawing nearer to God and of being more like Messiah. We can practice the presence of God by praying the traditional *b'rakhot* as Yeshua did. And as God touches our hearts and surprises us with his bounties and his love, why should we not coin our own spontaneous *b'rakhot*?

For Thought

God planned the time, place, and culture into which he sent his Son. He does the same for all his children.

Sometimes everything I do seems to go wrong. I am at odds with myself, the world around me, and God. Yet, surely there is no need for me to feel that I am out of place—a square peg in a round hole. What

God made me is what he meant me to be. Where he put me is where he meant me to be. Sometimes this is hard to accept, but not to do so is to resist God.

Perhaps I feel that I could accomplish more for the Lord "if only." If only I had gifts like that other person. If only I had better health. If only I could live in a better house or neighborhood. If only my family was more sympathetic. If only I was not married to him (or her). If only, if only, if only!

Yeshua wasted no energy on "if onlys." He had no regrets about who he was. He willingly trod the path on which the Father had set him, spending himself to the uttermost.

God's hands are sure hands. He makes no mistakes. When God made me, he did not get it wrong! As a skilled jeweler chooses just the right setting for a precious gem, so God chose the right environment in which to place me. I can feel utterly secure in his choice.

> For you fashioned my inmost being,
> you knit me together in my mother's womb.
> I thank you because I am awesomely made,
> wonderfully; your works are wonders—
> I know this very well.
> My bones were not hidden from you
> when I was being made in secret,
> intricately woven in the depths of the earth.
> Your eyes could see me as an embryo,
> but in your book all my days were already written;
> my days had been shaped
> before any of them existed. (Ps. 139:13–16)

A Prayer

Lord, I thank you for your sure hands in forming me. Your loving heart has made me what I am. Your perfect wisdom has brought me to where I am today. I freely offer everything that I am and everything that I have to you, even as my Messiah Yeshua taught in his words, his life, and his death.

Blessed are you, O Lord our God, King of the universe, who does all things well.

Bless the Lord
for Who He Is

Chapter 2

Blessed Are You

—

ברוך אתה
Barukh Atah

—

The *b'rakhot* have a standard structure. Every traditional *b'rakhah* begins with the same three elements. The first is called the *Barukh*: "Blessed are you." The second element is called the *Shem*: "O Lord our God." The final element is called the *Malkhut*: "King of the universe."

In this chapter, we will look at the *Barukh*, while in the next two chapters we will examine more closely the *Shem* and the *Malkhut*.

The *Barukh*

The word *barukh* means "bless." But what does it mean to "bless the Lord"? Isn't a blessing something that God bestows upon us? Doesn't the word "bless" imply the graciousness of a greater party toward a lesser? How can I possibly "bless" the Lord? What arrogance! Shouldn't we use the word "praise" in this context?

Indeed, some Bible translations do use "praise" rather than "bless." However, is it not a presumption to change the wording of Scripture simply because we do not understand how it can mean what it says? Is it not better to wrestle with the text as a humble learner than to approach it with a ready-made theology into which every idea must fit? That is like making the frame before painting the picture, so that the dimensions of the frame dictate the size of the picture! I would rather gaze in awe and wonder as God reveals the picture more fully, then make my theology as a frame.

The Meaning of *Barakh*

The root meaning of the Hebrew word *barakh* is to "kneel" or to "bless." That eliminates any presupposition that a blessing can only be conveyed to the lesser by the greater. If we associate blessing with kneeling, then I can give as well as receive it. I may even bless God, for I can certainly kneel before him. There is no contradiction between our smallness in relation to the great God and the call upon us to bless the Lord. That call pervades the Psalms. David, giving his final directions to the people, ordered them to bless *Adonai* their God. "All the community blessed ADONAI, the God of their ancestors, bowing their heads and prostrating themselves before ADONAI and before the king" (1 Chron. 29:20). The key for me, then, is that when I bless God, I do so on my knees (at least metaphorically), acknowledging who he is, what he has done, and how much I owe him.

Psalms 103 and 104 do just that. Kidner said of this pair of Psalms, "In the galaxy of the Psalter these are twin stars of the first magnitude" (Kidner 364). The psalmist praises God for the benefits he received personally (103:3–5) and those given to the nation throughout its history (103:6–12). He is affirming God's unchanging character of *chesed,* or merciful, compassionate love (103:13–18). He is proclaiming the majesty of God's eternal kingship (103:19–22). He is marveling at God's self-revelation in the wonders of natural creation (104:1–32). How does one respond to such a God? What can I offer in return that is remotely comparable in value? I have nothing to give. All I can do is fall on my knees in humble adoration. I can sing praise to him as well as I am able (104:33), meditate on the inexhaustible riches of who he is and what he has done (104:34), and rejoice in him (104:34). In short, I can bless him (104:35).

Blessing God in Traditional Jewish Practice

The idea of blessing God is not foreign to Judaism. The *b'rakhot* punctuate the life of the practicing Jewish person in response to both routine and special occurrences. In many cases, it seems that the word "bless" is the same as "thank." Nothing good ought to be received without a *b'rakhah*—a worshipful giving of thanks. Indeed, such an omission is equivalent to robbing God (Hirsch 526). For instance, after a meal, the "grace" may be "Let us bless him of whose bounty we have partaken." That is close to the common Christian wording, "Let us give thanks." In the synagogue, those called up to the reading of *Torah* (the first five books of the Bible) say this blessing: "Bless ye the Lord, who is to be blessed." The congregation responds: "Blessed be the Lord, who is to be blessed forever and ever."

Blessing God can be an act of submission. In blessing, I am saying, "Here I am, Lord, entirely available to be used for the furtherance of your purposes. I only want to do your will." So Hirsch stated, "Whenever you say to God: 'Blessed art Thou . . .' you subject all the powers of your being to the fulfilment of the Divine will" (Hirsch 475). The *b'rakhah* is not just a form of words or even an expression of gratitude but something much deeper and infinitely more demanding. The Hebrew word *nefesh* (soul) refers to the whole personality, the total being. Therefore, when I say "Bless the Lord, my soul," I am laying everything I am at his feet to serve his purposes.

Believers in Yeshua are challenged to attain the same level of self-giving. In response to who he is and what he has done (Rom. 11:33–36), the Scriptures exhort us to offer ourselves "as a sacrifice, living and set apart for God. This will please him; it is the logical 'Temple worship' for you" (Rom. 12:1). Yeshua came to do his Father's will, ultimately kneeling in the garden and saying, "Not what I want, but what you want!" (Matt. 26:39). The making of a *b'rakhah* is a verbal affirmation of discipleship.

God Is Blessed

Another interpretation of "*Barukh atah*" can be that we are saying, not "May God be blessed," but "God *is* blessed." So the *b'rakhah* becomes a statement of who God is.

Similarly, one can interpret the meaning as "You are the source of all blessings." Thus, says Binyamin Forst, the *b'rakhah* "becomes a testimony of man's total dependence upon God for all that he has" (Forst 27).

The Talmud tells of a Rabbi Ishmael ben Elisha, a priest, who saw God as he was ministering in the Temple. God said to him, "Ishmael my son, bless me."

Ishmael responded, "May it be thy will that thy mercy may subdue thy wrath; and may thy mercy prevail over thy attributes, so that thou mayest deal with thy children in the quality of mercy and enter on their behalf within the line of strict justice."

Now that, at first sight, does not look like a blessing. Yet the passage continues: "And he nodded his head towards me." In other words, God did indeed accept Ishmael's expression of dependence upon him, for mercy and blessing, as a *b'rakhah* (*Ber.* 7a).

The *B'rakhah* as a Prayer

The *b'rakhah* may be a prayer as well as a statement of faith and submission. As such, it calls for a response from God. Forst expresses it like this: "The *b'racha* thus creates a new reality—one in which the blessings from the Infinite Source may descend upon the one who has uttered the *b'racha*" (Forst 29). This means that in saying the *b'rakhah* we are acting creatively, participating in making the blessing a reality. That expression of utter dependence is necessary before God's blessing can flow to us. This is why, Forst says, we "make," rather than "say," a *b'rakhah*.

Rav Shimi explained the words "Bless the Lord, O my soul" like this:

> Just as the Holy One, blessed be he, fills the whole world, so the soul fills the body. Just as the Holy One, blessed be he, sees but is not seen, so the soul sees, but is not itself seen. Just as the Holy One, blessed be he, feeds the whole world, so the soul feeds the whole body. Just as the Holy One, blessed be he, is pure, so the soul is pure. Just as the Holy One, blessed be he, abides in the innermost precincts, so the soul abides in the innermost precincts. Let that which has these five qualities come and praise him who has these five qualities. (*Ber.* 10a)

This represents a typical talmudic approach to biblical exegesis. One takes the text at face value, examines it, discusses it, dissects it, and elaborates on it. Layer upon layer of meaning—some obvious, some bewildering to the non-talmudic scholar—is uncovered. By these means, the scholar will come to some conclusion.

So, How Can We Bless God?

It is still amazing that an omnipotent, infinite, and eternal God can desire to receive our blessing. How can he see us as having any significance? Why does it matter to him whether we bless him or not? Forst suggests that the answer lies in relationship, and every relationship requires communication. When we make a *b'rakhah*, we are affirming that the relationship we have with God is one that he has forged. The relationship is dependent upon his goodwill, for without that goodwill, we would be utterly alone and destitute. "A *b'racha* binds man forever to an everlasting God" (Forst 24).

God expects his people to bless him. In his farewell address to Israel, Moses reminded the people of all that God had done for them. In the years ahead, they were never to forget his provision. "You will eat and be satisfied, and you will bless *Adonai* your God for the good land he has given you" (Deut. 8:10).

Remembering is a vital ingredient of Judaism. In the *Tanakh* and the traditions, there are constant reminders of what God has done in the past. He is never just the Creator God; he is always the One who "brought us up out of the land of Egypt, out of the house of bondage." He is the God who chose to be in relationship to with his people. The *b'rakhot* help us to remember that.

Remembering to Bless

"Remembering" was important to Yeshua, as it is to the Jewish people. Celebrating the Passover *seder* with his disciples, he broke the *afikomen* (the portion of unleavened bread eaten after the meal) and said, "This is my body . . . ; do this in memory of me" (Luke 22:19). The *seder* was then, as it still is, an act of remembrance. At its institution God had said, "This will be a day for you to remember and celebrate" (Exod. 12:14). Yeshua was adding another layer of remembrance. As we celebrate the ancient national deliverance from Egypt, we are to bless and remember him, our personal deliverer.

For Thought

I readily remember the hurts and offenses I have suffered. But perhaps the next time I find myself dwelling on these things I can turn my thoughts to remember Yeshua—what he did for me, what it cost him. How paltry my pain seems in light of the price he paid!

Bless *Adonai*, my soul!
Everything in me, bless his holy name!
Bless *Adonai*, my soul,
and forget none of his benefits!

He forgives all your offenses,
he heals all your diseases,
he redeems your life from the pit,
he surrounds you with grace and compassion,
he contents you with good as long as you live,
so that your youth is renewed like an eagle's.

Bless *Adonai*, my soul! (Ps. 103:1–5, 22)

A Prayer

Lord, as I remember who you are, I kneel before you in humble adoration. As I remember all that you have done for me, I can only say, "Thank you, bless you."

Blessed are you, O Lord our God, King of the universe, who sent his only and unique Son, so that everyone who trusts in him may have eternal life.

Chapter 3

O Lord Our God

—

יי אלהינו
Adonai Eloheynu

—

"Without mention of God's Name and kingship a blessing is no blessing" (*Ber.* 40b). These words are a response to the words in the Song of Moses: "I will proclaim the name of ADONAI. Come, declare the greatness of our God" (Deut. 32:3).

The second part of the structure of the b'rakhot is the *Shem* (Name): "O Lord our God." In blessing God, we acknowledge who he is.

The *Shem*

A *b'rakhah* will usually begin with the words "Blessed are you, O Lord our God, King of the universe." Then will follow words appropriate to the occasion. Only in the case of blessings not laid down by the sages do we omit the words "O Lord our God, King of the universe" (Friedlander 444). We cannot separate the Lord from his Name or his Kingdom. That is why the reciting of the *Sh'ma* concludes with the words "Blessed be his Name, whose Kingdom is forever and ever." Rabbi Binyamin Forst states that one of the seven specific names of *haShem* (the Name) must be used in the prefix to a *b'rakhah*. These are (1) the Tetragrammaton (the ineffable Name of four letters—יהוה); (2) *Adonai* (Lord); (3) *El* (God); (4) *Elohim* or *Eloheynu* (Our Lord); (5) *Eh'yeh* (I AM); (6) *Shaddai* (Almighty); (7) *Adonai Tzva'ot* (The Lord of Hosts) (Forst 40).

An Ancient Custom

The custom of blessing the Lord goes back a long way. Abraham's servant believed that God had led him directly to the house of his master's relatives. He responded to his good fortune by exclaiming, "Blessed be ADONAI, God of my master Avraham, who has not abandoned his faithful love for my master" (Gen. 24:27). When Moses' father-in-law, Jethro, visited him after the Exodus from Egypt, he rejoiced with Israel in their deliverance with the words "Blessed be ADONAI, who has rescued you from the Egyptians and from Pharaoh" (Exod. 18:10). When Ruth gave birth to a son, the women rejoiced with Naomi, saying, "Blessed be ADONAI, who today has provided you a redeemer!" (Ruth 4:14). Abigail met David with appeasement after her husband had insulted him. David gave her honor but credited the Lord with keeping him from violent revenge. "Blessed be ADONAI the God of Isra'el, who sent you today to meet me" (1 Sam. 25:32). David's expression of confidence in God's faithfulness is "Blessed be ADONAI, for he heard my voice as I prayed for mercy" (Ps. 28:6). There are other biblical examples. The wording is "*Barukh YHVH*," always pronounced (out of respect) as "*ADONAI*," or the LORD.

Sometimes, we encounter the slightly different form "*Barukh atah Adonai*" ("Blessed are you, O Lord"). David used these words in his prayer of delight after the people's generous giving for the building of the Temple: "Blessed be you, ADONAI, the God of Isra'el our father, forever and ever" (1 Chron. 29:10). Again, in Psalm 119, the psalmist exclaimed, "Blessed are you, ADONAI! Teach me your laws" (v. 12). This form is also found in intertestamental writings.

The Jewish Encyclopedia states, "In the time of Ezra worship was begun with the call: '*Bareku et Adonay*,' each thanksgiving being followed by the congregational response: AMEN or *Baruk* . . . Amen" ("Benedictions"). Examples of this form appear in Psalms 41:14, 72:18–19, and 106:48. This is why each separate thanksgiving in the service is called a *b'rakhah*. Most of the *b'rakhot* were established around the year 350 B.C.E. by the men of the Great Assembly (Forst 35).

For Whose Benefit?

We offer a *b'rakhah* primarily for God's sake, not our own. This is why the opening words are always an expression of belief in God as the only Ruler of the universe and the supreme One to whom we owe submission and allegiance. Similarly, Maimonides' Fifth Principle states, "It is He (be He exalted) who must be worshipped, aggrandized, and made known by His greatness and obedience shown to Him" (Jacobs, *Principles* 149).

B'rakhot are a means of worship. "God wants man to worship Him because only in this way can man reach out to the divine, be

aware of God's presence and His majesty, and become God-like"
(Jacobs, *Principles* 155). They are a way of giving pleasure to God.
They are also a form of prayer, and "God desires man to express his
love of him, dependence on him and wish to commune with him"
(Jacobs, *Principles* 150).

Hasidism developed in the eighteenth century to combat the perceived dryness of contemporary rabbinical Judaism. The members of
this sect believe that one may worship with enthusiasm and joy, expressing devotion, love, and piety. The Bratzlaver, a Hasidic rabbi of the
eighteenth and nineteenth centuries, expressed such a view of prayer
poetically: "Every word of your prayer is like a rose which you pick
from its bush. You continue until you have formed a bouquet, a complete blessing. From them you form new bouquets of blessings, until
you have pleated a wreath of glory unto the Lord" (Newman 337).
Imagine that every time you make a *b'rakhah* you are offering a beautiful, fragrant bouquet to your beloved! Hence, the *b'rakhah* is an expression of the way we see ourselves in relation to God. He is divine, and we
approach him not only with gratitude and love but also with awe and
reverence (Forst 26).

Some *b'rakhot* are recited regularly as a part of the synagogue
services and daily prayers. Some are used only on special occasions. Because they embody an affirmation of who God is, they are an
expression of Maimonides' Fifth Principle:

> I believe with perfect faith that to the Creator, blessed be his
> Name, and to him alone it is right to pray, and that it is not
> right to pray to any being besides him.

Some rabbis considered the making of *b'rakhot* to be a personal and intimate experience. Eliezer of Worms taught that one should say the
words *Blessed art Thou* "as if a man were conversing with his neighbor"
(Jacobs, *Jewish Mystics* 49). Each *b'rakhah* is prayer in its highest form,
in that it moves from acknowledging God to expressing appreciation of
his acts and only then to asking—or intimating—that God might help
the worshiper in his or her immediate situation of need. It is right that
we should praise him with an attitude of adoration for all that he is—
for his infinite wisdom, his power, and his love. It is also fitting that we
should "thank Him in gratitude for all the good things He lavishes
upon us" (Epstein 132). Many believers do this in a general way. How
much better to give spontaneous, specific thanks "for any pleasure we
enjoy in life, whether through food, drink, wonderful sights, or delightful odours" (Epstein 133).

B'rakhot in the Whole of Life

The *b'rakhot* are a constant reminder that no area of life exists apart from God. We are to consecrate our whole lives to him in whose eyes all is holy. That will help us to fill our minds with thoughts of God and keep our steps in the ways of righteousness. Then whatever the godly do becomes a holy act. When we enjoy a good meal, we perform an act of holiness. When we gladden our heart with a cup of wine, we perform an act of holiness. Our joys and pleasures, our leisure, our recreations, our games, our holidays are all acts of holiness. They all form part of holy living (Epstein 69). It is helpful to remember that no area of our lives is "secular" as opposed to "spiritual." We do not live our lives in separate compartments, in which the values of the one have no relevance in the domain of the other. "*B'rachos* play a vital role in hallowing the ordinary and the mundane by declaring that godliness is relevant to all that we do" (Forst 25).

The *b'rakhot* remind us of our dependence on God. Everything for which we make a *b'rakhah* comes from him. "One cannot say '*Shehakol ni'hiyeh bidvaro*' [by whose word all things are made] with *kavana* [intent, concentration] and simultaneously cling to the belief that . . . it was my own strength and personal power that brought me all this prosperity" (Forst 23). As we focus on our utter dependence on God, we come to feel a deep sense of gratitude for all the good things he showers upon us. The word *barukh* is much more than "thank you." It is a recognition of all that God is to us and all he has done for us. We are profoundly indebted to and dependent upon God.

An Expression of Relationship

Ultimately, a *b'rakhah* is an expression of relationship. Rabbi Forst points out that it is possible to walk away from a simple "thank you." We have done our duty, so to speak, and may now move on to other things. The sense of indebtedness has cleared. Making a *b'rakhah* is different. We have declared faith in, dependence upon, and allegiance to Almighty God. The debt to him is ongoing; it can never be cleared.

We do not have a benefactor who performed a one-time *mitzvah* but one who ties us to himself in an unbreakable relationship. The *b'rakhah* "binds man forever to an everlasting God" (Forst 24). That is the relationship reflected in the laws and practice of the *b'rakhot*.

Yeshua constantly reminded his followers that they were bound in relationship to a loving heavenly Father. The relationship is one in which he, the Almighty, whose name and character are holy and totally "other," would never forget, never cease to care, never refuse to hear. Yet, this relationship was one in which Yeshua's *talmidim* (disciples) should always approach God with awe and respect.

In what Christians commonly refer to as the "Lord's Prayer," Yeshua encourages us to pray, "Our Father . . ." God is dear to us as a parent. But he is also "in heaven" and we are to pray, "May your Name be kept holy" (Matt. 6:9–10). This is what it is like when one has a relationship with a divine being. This is why we bless him every day.

For Thought

Sometimes we are casual in our attitude to God. We come to him when we feel like it. We expect him to do what we want when we want, and we may be thrown off course when he does not do as we ask. Respect and awe may be alien concepts to us. However, we can allow God to change our way of seeing things. He can renew the warped lenses of our eyes so that we see him as he is.

Adonai! Our Lord! How glorious
is your name throughout the earth! . . .

When I look at your heavens, the work of your fingers,
the moon and stars that you set in place—
what are mere mortals, that you concern yourself with them;
humans, that you watch over them with such care?
  (Psalm 8:2, 4–5[1, 3–4])

A Prayer

Lord, I marvel that you, who inhabit eternity, feel concern for me. You are almighty, unique. You are God. Yet, I matter to you. I bow before you in humble adoration.

Blessed are you, O Lord. You are my Lord; you are my God.

Chapter 4

King of the Universe

—

מלך העולם
Melekh Ha'Olam

—

"Beside thee we have no king, who redeemeth and saveth, setteth forth and delivereth . . . yea, we have no king but Thee" (*Pes.* 18a). We affirm this, the *Birkat Hashir* (Blessing of Song), frequently in synagogue worship and most notably, near the end of every Passover *seder*. In this way, we proclaim it to be God's initiative that has enabled his people in their most notable achievements. We address God as "King of the Universe" in the third part of the *B'rakhot*, namely the *Malkhut*.

The *Malkhut* in the *Tanakh*

Many kings lorded their power over the Jewish people. Some kings were of Israel's choosing; most were not. Israel's experience of human rulers has been much as God foretold through Samuel, when the ancient Israelites rejected the Lord as King (1 Sam. 8). Through much hardship, the Jewish people have learned that *Adonai* is the only true King; he has their well-being at heart and he rules in righteousness and justice.

The biblical writers offered a highly developed view of the kingship of God. He is the King of all the earth (Ps. 47:2–3[1–2]), the King of all creation (95:3–5), the King forever (10:16), and the King of glory (24:8). Isaiah called him "Ya'akov's king" (41:21). Zephaniah referred to him as "the king of Isra'el" (3:15). The later prophets foresaw a time when *Adonai Tzva'ot* (the Lord of hosts) will be seen as the great and universal King (Zech. 14:17; Mal. 1:14). Yet, his kingship is also personally meaningful to me—he is *my* King (Ps. 44:4–5[3–4]).

This comprehensive view of the Lord as King—infinite, eternal, universal, yet also present and personal—has characterized the Jewish attitude toward him through the ages.

The *Malkhut* in Jewish Tradition

Every Friday night, practicing Jewish people sing *Shalom aleykhem*—"Peace be to you, ministering angels, messengers of the Most High, of the supreme Sovereign" (*Siddur Lev Chadash* 76). This is a song of welcome to the messengers of the sovereign King of kings, sung at the coming in of Shabbat (Sabbath). Likewise, in the synagogue, worshipers proclaim, "Thine, O Lord, is the kingdom, and the supremacy, as head over all" (*ADP* 80). That high view, however, is qualified. "Kingship with reference to the Deity indicates nothing more than the aspect of majesty; and any thought of autocratic exclusion is removed by the frequent addition of 'our Father' to 'our King' " (*ADP* 45). The relationship is personal, intimate. God the King is not only distant and unapproachable; he is also our Father—close, concerned. He is the God who revealed himself to Moses: "I have seen . . . and heard . . . I know their pain . . . I have come down to rescue them" (Exod. 3:7–8).

As part of the *Sh'ma* (see Deut. 6:4), we say, "Blessed be his Name, whose glorious kingdom is forever and ever." He is our Lord, our God, and our King—forever.

The *Malkhut* Today

How does such a view of God's kingship affect us? First, it means that we come to him with an attitude of respect and awe. "We bend the knee and offer worship and thanks before the supreme King of kings, the Holy One, blessed be he . . . the seat of whose glory is in the heavens above, and the abode of whose might is in the loftiest heights. He is our God; there is none else: in truth he is our King; there is none besides him" (*Aleynu* prayer, *ADP* 169).

It means, too, that we should live our lives in submission to the King. The Talmud defines the recital of the *Sh'ma* as "the acceptance of the yoke of the Kingdom of Heaven" (*Ber.* 14b). That means submission to the divine discipleship (Cohen 4). A kingdom is, before all else, the place where the monarch reigns.

Relationship with the King

The rabbis have instructed us to "vie one with the other in the fear of God and practice loving deeds towards one another" (*Sifre Deut.* para. 323; 138b). Accepting the yoke of the kingdom implies accepting the yoke of the commandments (*Ber.* 14b). We will one day have to render account to the King of the way we have carried out his orders (Epstein 86). Kingdom living, then, must color the whole of life and all our relationships. That is why the practices of *tzedakah* (righteousness, charity) and *mitzvot* (commandments, good deeds) are important aspects of Jewish life. The King we serve loves righteousness and judgment (*Ber.* 12b). Our unrighteousness is unacceptable to him. On the eve of *Yom HaKippurim* (the Day of Atonement), in the service known as *Kol Nidre* (All Vows), we have traditionally brought the most comprehensive confession imaginable, addressing it to "our Father, our King." The sounding of the *shofar* (ram's horn) on Rosh HaShanah (New Year), the first of the Days of Awe and Repentance, is a proclamation of the kingship of God. On that day, Psalm 47 is read: "Sing praises to our king, sing praises! . . . For God is king of all the earth. . . . God rules the nations; God sits on his holy throne." According to the Talmud, God said, "Proclaim me King over you . . . so that your remembrance may rise favorably before Me; and through what? Through the blowing of the *shofar*" (*Rosh Hashanah* 16a).

We therefore approach him our Father, our King—in an attitude of submission, wishing to dedicate ourselves to his service. That is his rightful due, for "all is His, and we are his people, and his servants" (*Ber.* 46b).

Messianic Kingship

Jewish thought has always associated kingship with the expected Messiah. Isaiah saw him as a descendant of King David (11:1). Ezekiel looked into the distant future and saw one nation, under one king, whom God described as "my servant David" (37:24). Zechariah was more explicit. The coming one would ride humbly into Jerusalem on a donkey, yet he is called "your king" and his coming would be cause for rejoicing (9:9).

Yeshua did not shrink from accepting the role of Messiah-King, though he described it in different terms from what had been expected. A kingdom not of this world? A kingdom within and among us? A king who must die? What kind of Messiah could this be? Yeshua's concept of heavenly has been alien to Jewish thinking. Klausner has expressed it like this: "The kingdom of the Jewish King-Messiah was, and remained . . . *a kingdom of this world*" (517).

Eventually, it was Yeshua's claim of kingship that the political leadership seized on as the excuse to get rid of Yeshua. They feared that Rome would see it as rebellion against the emperor. However, a major part of Yeshua's teaching was revealing to his disciples an unfamiliar, even alien, aspect of messianic kingship. The Kingdom of Heaven belongs to those who not only perform righteous acts, but also experience persecution for so doing (Matt. 5:10). The Kingdom is like a small seed that needs to be nurtured (Matt. 13:31–32), like yeast that spreads invisibly (Matt. 13:33), like hidden treasure (Matt. 13:44). In this Kingdom, human values and priorities are overturned (Matt. 18:1–4).

Yochanan (John) saw no contradiction in the sacrificed Lamb being addressed as "Lord of lords and King of kings" both in heaven and on earth (Rev. 17:14; 19:16). One day all humankind will see him reigning forever. His kingship is glorious. However, his is a glory that springs from servanthood and sacrifice. It will be just as the prophets foretold.

For Thought

We join with *Sha'ul* (Paul) in waiting for the appearance of our Lord—*Yeshua haMashiach.* "His appearing will be brought about in its own time by the blessed and sole Sovereign, who is King of kings and Lord of lords" (1 Tim. 6:15). But what about today? When we pray, "Your kingdom come," we draw upon the riches of Jewish tradition. We approach God in awe of his majesty and involvement in our personal lives. Our King calls us to follow him as servants, living sacrificial lives before him and in relationship with one another.

> Lord of the world, King supreme
> Before anything was formed, He alone reigned.
> When by His will all things were created,
> His sovereign name was made known.

> And at the end, when all things cease to be,
> The exalted God alone will still be King.
> He was, and He is,
> and He will be forever glorious.
> (*Adon Olam*, traditional song, qtd. in Budoff 32)

A Prayer

Our Father, our King, we have sinned before you. Our relationships are too often marred by jealousies and rivalries. O Lord, hear. O Lord, forgive. Our Father, our King, hasten the day when Israel returns to you as King. Our Father, our King, reign within and among your people in the Messiah. My Father, my King, I find it difficult to walk humbly with you. It is even harder to walk humbly with others, in servanthood, as Yeshua did and as you call me to do. O Lord, hear. O Lord, forgive. My Father, my King, grow the seed of your kingdom in me. Reign alone and unchallenged in my life.

Blessed are you, our Father, our King.

Bless the Lord
for What He Has Done

Chapter 5

By Day, By Night

—

ביום בלילה
BaYom—BaLailah

—

"Blessed be the Lord by day, blessed be the Lord by night," we pray from the *Authorised Daily Prayer Book*; "blessed be the Lord when we lie down, blessed be the Lord when we rise up" (295). Our daily lives, from beginning to end, are to be God-centered. As we awake, we offer ourselves—our gifts, our powers—to him. We resolve to honor him in all that the day might bring. Throughout the day, we encounter numerous opportunities to bless God for his greatness, his wisdom, and his compassion. Then, at the day's end, we give back to him our whole being (Hirsch 524).

Blessings have been formulated to cover almost any eventuality that may arise. From the day's beginning to its ending, we are conscious of the presence of God. Hence, we endeavor to express appropriate feelings toward him. The day begins with this prayer:

> O my God, the soul which you have given me is pure. You created it within me, you breathed it into me. You preserve it within me and you will take it from me, but will restore it to me hereafter. So long as the soul is within me, I will give thanks to you, O Lord my God and God of my fathers, Sovereign of all worlds, Lord of all souls. Blessed are you, O Lord, who restores souls unto dead bodies. (*Ber.* 60b)

In other words, according to Jewish teaching, our souls are inherently pure. Disciples of Yeshua might have problems saying that particular *b'rakhah* without some qualification! Nevertheless, it is a good principle to practice the presence of God from the first waking moment. The day ends with the following words:

Blessed are you, O Lord our God, King of the universe, who makes the bands of sleep to fall upon my eyes, and slumber upon my eyelids, and gives light to the apple of the eye. May it be your will, O Lord my God, to suffer me to lie down in peace . . . let not evil dreams and lustful thoughts trouble me; and let my bed be perfect before you, and give light to my eyes, lest I sleep the sleep of death. Blessed are you, O Lord, who gives light to the whole world in your glory. (*Ber.* 60b)

"From the time we awake in the morning till the evening when we lie down to sleep, there is not a moment that fails to bring to our knowledge some Divine act of kindness towards us" (Friedlander 283). How good it would be to live life in such a way, always seeking opportunities to bless God! It would transform our quality of life.

The Daily Devotional Life

The *Sh'ma* is the central statement of faith for the Jewish people. Before reciting it in the morning, one blesses God for the regular sequence of light and darkness. Afterward, one proclaims, "Blessed be his glorious Name, forever and ever." Before the reading of *Torah*, one may say, "Blessed are you, O Lord our God, King of the universe, who has chosen us from all nations and given us your *Torah*. Blessed are you, O Lord, who gives the Torah" (*Ber.* 11b). Afterward, the blessing is this:

Blessed are you, O Lord our God, King of the universe, who has given us the Torah of truth and planted everlasting life in our midst. Blessed are you, O Lord, who gives Torah. (*ADP* 68)

Before and after the reading of the *Haftarah* (Prophets), we bless the Lord for those words of comfort and of messianic hope. "Soon may he come and rejoice our hearts. . . . Blessed art thou, O Lord, the Shield of David" (*ADP* 49). Before and after the reading of the Psalms, we bless God as the One who is worthy of our praise: "Blessed be thou, O Lord, who art extolled by praises." Every daily service includes the עשרה שמונה (*Shemoneh Esreh*—Eighteen Blessings), known as the עמידה (*Amidah*—Standing Prayer). We will be looking at the *Amidah* in later chapters.

Everything Reminds Us of God

The range of *b'rakhot* is truly amazing. For example, there are *b'rakhot* to recite before performing a *mitzvah* (a commandment), beginning with the words "Blessed are you, O Lord our God, King of the universe, who has commanded us to . . ." This is the form used at the ritual washing of hands and at the lighting of lights on Shabbat and festivals. Interestingly, one is not required to make a *b'rakhah* before performing a work of charity, which is also a *mitzvah*. Why not? Because, explained Rabbi Bunam, we might make the excuse that we are not clean enough to make the *b'rakhah* and so evade performing the *mitzvah* (Newman 35). What a realistic understanding of human nature! There are blessings associated with eating and drinking, seeing a remarkable sight, sensing an agreeable smell, and attending a special occasion. After deliverance from danger, one may say, "Blessed be the Lord, who bestows benefits on the undeserving." On hearing good news, the wording is "Blessed are you who are good and dispenses good." There is even a blessing with which to respond to bad news: "Blessed are you, the true judge." There is a formula, too, for blessing God when one receives a benefit (such as rainfall) that will also aid others: "Blessed is He who is good and does good" (Steinsaltz 182).

A Privilege, Not a Burden

According to Rabbi Meir (see introduction), one should say a hundred blessings every day. That would seem to be an awesome burden. Not so, says Binyamin Forst; it is no burdensome duty but a privilege (Forst 36). Everything we receive is a gift from the almighty, loving God, "a divine miracle enclothed in nature" (Ginsburgh 293). The *b'rakhot*, Forst says, "provide eloquent testimony that each moment of our lives and the entirety of our being are inextricably tied to God's will" (36). Making the *b'rakhot* in sincerity reinforces our consciousness of God. We ought not to experience or enjoy anything without an acknowledgment that God is the Creator and source of all.

The Sacred and the Secular

In Hebrew thinking there is no separation between sacred and secular deeds. The most mundane, the most earthy and basic functions and actions are performed in God's sight. They are not unmentionable before him. Hence the following:

> Blessed art thou, O Lord our God, King of the universe, who has formed man in wisdom and created in him many orifices and vessels. It is revealed and known before the throne of thy glory, that if one of these be opened, or one of those be closed,

it would be impossible to exist and to stand before thee. Blessed art thou, O Lord, who healest all flesh and doest wondrously. (*ADP* 4)

This prayer, known as the *Asher Yatzar* (literally, "who fashioned") is the *b'rakhah* one makes upon leaving the rest room!

Yeshua and the *B'rakhot*

The diverse *b'rakhot* were part of the culture within which Yeshua grew to manhood. He would have blessed God when his body was functioning normally. Did he perhaps look at that crowd of five thousand hungry people and quietly make the *b'rakhah*: "Blessed are you, O Lord our God, King of the universe, who knows the secret minds of men" (Montefiore and Loewe 457)? He knew what was in people's hearts. From infancy, he must have learned the *Sh'ma* and the *b'rakhot*, so that they were an integral part of his life. Surely it is unthinkable that he and his disciples did not say a *b'rakhah* after the calming of the storm. They may have said something like "Blessed are you who bestows benefits on the undeserving," perhaps thinking of Psalm 107 as they did so.

For Thought

How was it that Yeshua was able to live such a difficult life with such poise and dignity? How could he could turn apparent failure into a task well finished, transforming crushed hopes into a new beginning? Yes, he was the Son of God, possessing unique abilities. Nevertheless, we can learn from his example. Life's irritations, disasters, injustices, and failures can become bridges to new opportunities.

The key is realizing Yeshua's total focus upon God. Nothing could daunt him, because he knew that nothing was outside God's control. If I really believe this for myself, then I will not fall to pieces when life seems to disintegrate. I will not carry a chip on my shoulder because someone has hurt me. Like Yeshua, I will have a serene certainty that God is able to use all circumstances for my blessing and his purposes. Even that hurtful act of injustice, that cruel stroke of misfortune, is God's will for my life.

Adonai, you have probed me, and you know me.
You know when I sit and when I stand up. . . .
You have hemmed me in both behind and in front
and laid your hand on me. . . .

God, how I prize your thoughts! . . .

Examine me, God, and know my heart;
test me, and know my thoughts.
See if there is in me any hurtful way,
and lead me along the eternal way. (Ps. 139:1–2, 5, 17, 23–24)

A Prayer

Lord, forgive me for being so easily distracted and disconcerted, for seeing obstacles where you have placed only stepping-stones. Give me the grace to be "in you," from the opening of my eyes in the morning to their closing at night. Only then will I learn to recognize, in the trials and tribulations of life, your wise guidance and your all-encompassing love.

Blessed are you, who are all good and who does only good.

Chapter 6

Who Brings Forth Bread from the Earth

—

המוציא לחם מן הארץ
HaMotzi Lekhem Min Ha'Aretz

—

"You will eat and be satisfied, and you will bless ADONAI your God for the good land he has given you," says Deuteronomy 8:10. The most common of all *b'rakhot* are those recited before and after eating. Discussion of these comprises the bulk of Tractate *B'rakhot*. There is a strong link between the eating of food and the history of the Jewish people, reflected in the saying "They tried to kill us; we won; let's eat." This further illustrates the truth that "the division between the physical and the spiritual in nature is illusory" (Forst 32).

Everything in his created world belongs to God by right. This includes the food we eat. Making a *b'rakhah* over food remind us of that fact and gives us an opportunity to express appropriate gratitude. Forst sees the *b'rakhah* as an act of redemption, required before we may consider the food ours, in partnership with God, and so be free to eat (Forst 131–132). He cites Psalm 115:16: "Heaven belongs to ADONAI, but the earth he has given to humankind." That is why the injunction has come down to us from the great Rabbi Akiba (second-century C.E. founder of Rabbinism): "A man is forbidden to taste anything without previously saying a benediction" (*Ber.* 35a). The only exceptions to this ruling are in the cases of food that has neither taste nor nutritional benefit (Forst 134) and food eaten in minute quantity—less than the size of an olive (Steinsaltz 173).

Blessings over Meals

Saying a blessing over a meal goes back at least as far as the days of Samuel. People would not expect to eat until a blessing had been offered over the sacrifice (1 Sam. 9:13). The words in Deuteronomy, quoted at the head of this chapter, point to a blessing being said after the meal as well. This is known as the *birkat ha'mazon* (grace after meals) and is quite lengthy, having three sections, each ending with a *b'rakhah*. The first section blesses God for his provision of sustenance for all creatures:

> Blessed art thou, O Lord our God, King of the universe, who feedest the whole world with thy goodness, with grace, with lovingkindness and tender mercy; thou givest food to all flesh. . . . Blessed art thou, O Lord, who givest food unto all. (*ADP* 280)

The second section blesses him for providing for the individual as well as for the nation of Israel. It remembers the Land, the Covenant, and the *Torah*:

> We thank thee, O Lord our God, because thou didst give as an heritage unto our fathers a desirable, good and ample land . . . as well as for thy covenant which thou hast sealed in our flesh, thy Law which thou hast taught us . . . and for the food wherewith thou dost constantly feed and sustain us on every day, in every season, at every hour. For all this, O Lord our God, we thank and bless thee. . . . Blessed art thou, O Lord, for the land and for the food. (*ADP* 280)

The third section is a prayer for the restoration of Jerusalem and the Temple. It looks to the coming of Messiah:

> Have mercy, O Lord our God, upon Israel thy people, upon Jerusalem thy city, upon Zion the abiding place of thy glory, upon the kingdom of the house of David thine anointed . . . and rebuild Jerusalem the holy city speedily in our days. Blessed art thou, O Lord, who in thy compassion rebuildest Jerusalem. (*ADP* 281)

Later, a fourth section was added. Here we bless God for his goodness and generosity:

Blessed art thou, O Lord our God, King of the universe, O God, our Father, our King, our Mighty One, our Creator, our Redeemer, our Maker, our Holy One, the Holy One of Jacob, our Shepherd, the Shepherd of Israel, O King, who art kind and dealest kindly with all. . . . May the All-merciful bless . . . us and all that is ours. . . . May he bless all of us together with a perfect blessing, and let us say, Amen. (*ADP* 283)

Tradition has it that the first section was instituted by Moses, the second by Joshua, the third by David and Solomon, and the fourth in Yavneh. Yavneh became Judaism's religious and national center after the destruction of the Temple (*Ber.* 48b). Most Christians say grace before meals. However, the practice of thanking God afterward is surely commendable. It reminds us of the lepers who came to Yeshua for healing, only one of whom returned afterward to give thanks (Luke 17:11–19). To make a *b'rakhah* before the meal may be an act of faith; to do so afterward is an act of acknowledgment and gratitude.

Specific Foods

Two *b'rakhot* are most frequently used in connection with food. For bread, one says:

Barukh atah, Adonai Eloheynu, Melech Ha'olam, hamotzi lekhem min ha'aretz (Blessed are you, O Lord our God, King of the universe, who brings forth bread from the earth).

For wine, the blessing is:

Barukh atah, Adonai Eloheynu, Melech Ha'olam, boray pri hagafen" (Blessed are you, O Lord our God, King of the Universe, who creates the fruit of the vine).

The two loaves on the Shabbat table are called *birchot* (blessings). They are the symbols of God's blessing in providing the double portion of manna in the desert. It is, therefore, as if we return blessing for blessing when we make the *b'rakhah* over bread on Shabbat.

A story is told concerning the familiar *Le Chayim* (To Life), which we often say before making the *b'rakhah* over wine. A *Hasid* asked a *tzaddik* (righteous man) why it was customary to say "Le Chayim" before reciting the benediction over a drink of wine. "The Tzaddik opened the Prayer Book and showed the Hasid the passage where we are enjoined to accept the Mitzvah of loving our neighbors before accepting the Mitzvah of loving God. The reason doubtless is that mortals need our love and sympathy more than God" (Newman 223–24).

There are a multitude of blessings, each for a different kind of food. The Tractate *B'rakhot* lists them. In order not to make a mistake, many people use the formula "*Shehakol nih'yeh b'dvaro*" (by whose word all things are made) when the food or drink in question is neither bread nor wine. The very strict, however, will say that one ought not to use this *b'rakhah* as an excuse for laziness. It is usually appropriate for all foods that do not grow from the earth, such as meat, eggs, milk, and water. Water occupies a unique place among the foods and drinks. It has neither taste nor nutritional value. However, presumably because of its necessity for life, it requires a *b'rakhah*—unless one is drinking it for a purpose other than to quench thirst. Such an occasion might be when one needs the water to swallow a pill (Forst 135).

A *b'rakhah* over food is not just a mechanical exercise; it is an expression of enjoyment—of gratitude to God for his bountiful provision. One should offer it, say the rabbis, with *kavanah*. Then it becomes "a part of one's overall dedication to a godly life" (Forst 33).

Yeshua Blessed Food

The Gospel records tell us that Yeshua made a *b'rakhah* over food as he was about to feed the five thousand (John 6:11) and again at the feeding of the four thousand (Matt. 15:36). Of course he did! At his last *seder* he took the *matzah* (unleavened bread), making a *b'rakhah* before breaking it. He said, "This is my body . . ." Then he took the third cup—the cup of redemption—and made the *b'rakhah* for wine, saying, "This is my blood . . ." Here we have one of the few occasions when we can say with certainty, "Yeshua made a *b'rakhah*." Generally, one may presume that Yeshua recited *b'rakhot* on customary occasions. If he had not done so, his omissions would have aroused comment. His perceived failure to perform *n'tilat yadayim* (the ritual washing of hands) appears to have done so (Mark 7:1–4).

Yeshua used the miraculous feeding of the five thousand to teach about himself. The people wondered, "How can he do such things?" Yeshua lifted the discussion onto a different plane, saying, "I am the bread which is life!" (John 6:35). The miracle demonstrated who he was. He claimed, "If anyone eats this bread, he will live forever. Furthermore, the bread that I will give is my own flesh" (6:51). In that final teaching session with the disciples before his arrest, Yeshua said, "I am the real vine" (John 15:1). The lifeblood of the vine drunk at the Passover *seder* symbolizes the lifeblood of the Messiah.

In addition to the bread and wine, Yeshua used water to demonstrate who he was: "Whoever drinks the water I will give him will never be thirsty again! On the contrary, the water I give him will become a spring of water inside him, welling up into eternal life!" (John 4:14). "Whoever puts his trust in me, . . . rivers of living water will flow from his inmost being!" (7:38).

For Thought

Yeshua did not just *give* bread; he *was* bread! He did not just *give* wine; he *was* the vine, the source of wine! He did not just *give* water; he *was* the fountain of water.

History tells us that if we employ the world's means to try to solve the world's problems, they will not be solved. Likewise, if I use the world's wisdom to solve my own personal problems, solutions will evade me. Yeshua promises that if we bring our hunger and our thirst to him, the true bread, the true water and wine, we will be fully and permanently satisfied.

"I am the bread which is life! Whoever comes to me will never go hungry, and whoever trusts in me will never be thirsty" (John 6:35).

A Prayer

Lord, give us this bread from now on (John 6:34).

Blessed are you, O Lord our God, King of the universe, who gives us, in Yeshua, all that we will ever need. In your compassion, you rebuild broken lives. You bless us, in Yeshua, with a perfect blessing.

Chapter 7

Concerning the Counting of the *Omer*

—

על ספירת העמר
Al S'firat Ha'Omer

—

"Blessed are you, O Lord our God, who has sanctified us by your commandments, and has commanded us to count the days of the Omer," we pray every year (*ADP* 270). This prayer is based on the practice described in Leviticus 23. Between the instructions dealing with *Pesach* (Passover) and those dealing with *Shavu'ot* (Pentecost), we find the words "You are to count seven full weeks . . . fifty days" (Lev. 23:15–16). On the day after the Shabbat in *Pesach* week (variously interpreted as the second day or as the Sunday in the festival week), a token offering of the barley harvest was to be brought—the *Omer*, which can mean a sheaf or a specified weight of grain. The counting was to begin on the day that offering—the *Reshit* (the first of the fruits)—was brought. It culminated in the feast of *Shavu'ot* (Weeks), or *Bikkurim* (Firstfruits), known to Christians as Pentecost (from the Greek word for fifty).

Orthodox Jews still do this counting, in obedience to the *Torah*. In some homes, a parchment scroll is turned to mark each day, adding to the above blessing the words "This is the . . . day [or week] of the *Omer*." The agricultural significance is still remembered: the *Reshit* is a token of the hoped-for harvest to come at *Shavu'ot*. Jewish people also remember that at this time the manna ceased to fall (Josh. 5:12). They pray that God will protect the harvest, and they express gratitude to the Lord of the harvest (Hertz, *Leviticus* 245).

The Meaning of *Shavu'ot*

Today, *Shavu'ot* is primarily seen as the commemoration of the giving of *Torah* at Sinai. In part, this may be a response to the Diaspora (the dispersion of the Jewish people following the destruction of the Temple

and Jerusalem). After the dispersion, it was no longer possible to celebrate the harvest in Israel at this time of year. Eric Lipson wrote, "The
Ten Words (Commandments) are read in synagogue, while everyone
stands. The child may receive his first lesson in Hebrew and religion.
Many will spend the first night in reading *Torah*, the Prophets, and rabbinical literature. Even the food eaten—honey and dairy dishes—
reminds us that *Torah* is as milk and honey to us" (unpublished).

The change of emphasis from agricultural to theological and national has affected the nation's attitude to the counting of the *Omer*.
Many now believe that this is the period when Israel was waiting for
God to give the supreme gift of *Torah* to his people. Above all, it is a period "dedicated to the honouring of the Torah . . . to remind all in
Israel, the bearers of the Torah, to be imbued with what is worthy and
good, of which they are the bearers" (Hirsch 123).

A Time of Mourning

The fifty days are also regarded as a period of mourning because of the
calamities that befell Israel at this season. During the Roman occupation, in the second century C.E., the great Rabbi Akiba supported the
revolt led by Bar Kochba. At that time, the story goes, a terrible plague
afflicted the disciples of Rabbi Akiba, and twenty-four thousand died.
The revolt failed, the Temple and Jerusalem were destroyed, and the
people were forced into exile. At this time of year, associated with the
harvest, Israel has been most reminded of that national disaster. It is no
longer possible to bring the required daily *Omer* to the Temple.

The fifty-day period is also a time of spiritual purification. These
weeks prepare the people to receive *Torah* (Ginsburgh 220). No weddings take place during the period. Even haircuts are forbidden. There
is a feeling of expectancy and solemnity, of waiting for something momentous to happen.

There is, however, a break in the mourning on the thirty-third
day—*Lag b'Omer*. This is traditionally recognized as the day on which
the manna first fell. It is also considered to be the day the plague lifted
from the disciples of Rabbi Akiba, so *Lag b'Omer* is sometimes called
the Scholars' Festival. It is also the day on which Bar Kochba tempo-
rarily recaptured Jerusalem. Rabbi Simeon ben Yochai, the second-
century C.E. scholar and mystic, died on this day. He, like Rabbi Akiba,
had openly defied the Roman edict against the study and teaching of
Torah. Forced to flee, he spent thirteen years in hiding. It seems his stu-
dents used to visit him once a year, always on the thirty-third day of the
Counting of the *Omer*. The day he died was "filled with endless joy and

with great light" (Koppelman Ross 93). That is why his disciples have celebrated the anniversary with song and dance through the centuries. Since then, the day has become a holiday, a break in the mourning, on which children have engaged in mock warfare with bows and arrows. Is this to recall the battle days of the Bar Kochba revolt? Is it to celebrate the rainbow that, according to tradition, appeared when Rabbi Simeon died? No one is sure.

The Link between Two Festivals

One thing is clear. The counting of the *Omer* links the festivals of *Pesach* and *Shavu'ot.* So strong is the linkage that many rabbis have seen the two as one festival. *Shavu'ot,* the festival of revelation, is the culmination of *Pesach,* the feast of deliverance. Indeed, *Shavu'ot* is also known as *Atzeret* (conclusion). Maimonides taught that the giving of *Torah* was the aim and object of the Exodus from Egypt (Hertz, *Leviticus* 247). Freedom was not an end in itself. Indeed, freedom without law (that is, direction) is of no real benefit. The redemption from Egypt is the central covenant reality for Israel, but "freedom acquires worth, reality, and meaning only through the principles of the Torah" (Hirsch 122).

Many have a mystical feeling about these weeks. "As Passover has poetically been called the day of Israel's betrothal to God, the Feast of Weeks would correspond to the wedding day . . . the counting of the Omer represents the longing of the bride for her wedding day . . . i.e. the longing of Israel for Divine Revelation" (Friedlander 394).

Waiting for the Father's Promise

This season was momentous for the infant Body of Messiah. All of the hopes of Yeshua's disciples were dashed as Messiah suffered and died. But they were euphoric after his Resurrection on the day of the *Reshit* offering in the Temple. Did they see any significance in the timing? Perhaps not immediately. Later, *Sha'ul* surely did, as he wrote to his Corinthian friends of the risen Messiah as the "firstfruits of those who have died"—the guarantee of the harvest to come (1 Cor. 15:20). Then they were left with instructions (again, picking up the tone of the *Omer* period) to wait (Acts 1:4). They were waiting for something else to happen, something that would complete Yeshua's work in them, something that would change them, give them power and direction. Now they would receive, not *Torah* only, but also the power to live it and to teach it. They would be able to fulfill the Messiah's commission: "You will receive power when the *Ruach haKodesh* comes upon you; you will be my witnesses both in Yerushalayim [Jerusalem] and in all Y'hudah [Judea] and Shomron [Samaria], indeed to the ends of the earth!" (Acts 1:8).

Surely, Yeshua was teaching them—and us—that salvation is not an end in itself. After Messiah's death and resurrection came the giving of the *Ruach haKodesh*. The full purpose of our salvation is that we may be empowered to serve and to be Messiah's witnesses to the nations, as Israel was meant to be. For that power we need, not only the *Torah*—God's Word—but also the writing of that Word on our hearts, as God dwells within us.

For Thought

The counting of the *Omer* suggests that *Pesach* and *Shavu'ot* are one festival. The one leads to the other. In the same way, our salvation becomes meaningful and complete as the Holy Spirit fills, transforms, and enables us. If we do not wish to belittle the price Messiah paid for us, we must accept God's whole purpose for our lives.

> Teach us to count our days,
> so that we will become wise. (Ps. 90:12)

Our waiting upon God must be purposeful—that he may change and empower us. "Wait for 'what the Father promised, which you heard about from me. . . . You will receive power when the *Ruach HaKodesh* comes upon you; you will be my witnesses . . . to the ends of the earth' " (Acts 1:4, 8).

A Prayer

Loving Father, teach me to wait patiently when days are dark and when light seems long in coming. Help me to look forward as well as to remember the past. Write your Word on my heart and keep me constantly filled with yourself so that I may be what you want me to be and do what you want me to do. Never let me be satisfied with things as they are in my walk with you.

Blessed are you who began a good work in me, and will carry it on to completion until the day of Messiah Yeshua (Phil. 1:6).

Chapter 8

Who Has Made the Creation

—

עשה מעשה בראשית

'Oseh Ma'aseh B'resheet

—

"Look for God on the stage of life, in Nature, and in the human world," advised Samson Hirsch, "resolving to dedicate yourself entirely to the Only One Who reveals Himself in such a God-filled world" (525). The creation reveals the Creator.

God, the Mind Behind Creation

You are driving along a narrow, winding, tree-enclosed road, steadily climbing. Each bend obscures the way ahead. You feel a sense of mystery, even oppression. Then, suddenly, it happens. You are on the crest of the hill; the trees melt away; beautiful landscape opens before you. Breathtaking! How can you not respond with a *b'rakhah*?

Judaism delights in finding opportunities to bless the Lord. Nature provides such opportunities in abundance, and there is a *b'rakhah* for every one. Sometimes we may witness a phenomenon for which there is no set *b'rakhah*. That is not a problem. "For shooting stars, earthquakes, thunders, storms, and lightnings one says, 'Blessed are you, O Lord our God, King of the universe, whose strength and might fill the world.' For mountains, hills, seas, rivers, and deserts one says, 'Blessed are you . . . who has made the creation' " (*Ber.* 54a). One never needs to be at a loss for a *b'rakhah*. That is true of Judaism in general, but particularly is it so of the Hasidic movement. One of the contributions of this movement has been to see, and rejoice in, God in all the beauties of nature. Its founder, the Baal Shem Tov (or Besht, an acronym), had an infectious gift for feeling and expressing delight in God's creation.

It has been a long journey to the seaside. Children are quarrelsome, parents exhausted by stories, quizzes, and games.

"Are we nearly there?"

"I'm bored!"

"Mom, I'm hungry!"

"I feel sick."

"Da-ad, she's annoying me!"

"He started it!"

Then—we are almost there. Arguments are suspended, irritations forgotten. It is the big moment. Who will see it first? Who will be the first to proclaim, "*Barukh atah Adonai, Eloheynu Melekh ha-olam, she asah et ha-yam ha-gadol*" ("Blessed are you, O Lord our God, King of the universe, who created the great sea")? "I said it first," shouts the triumphant one. Now the vacation can really begin, with the joyous reminder that God's is the hand that shaped creation.

The Creative Power of God's Word

Any fresh confrontation with the wonder of creation may stimulate a *b'rakhah*, perhaps "Blessed is he who spoke and the world came into existence." We rejoice in a God so great that he brought creation into being just by his word: "God said, 'Let there be . . .'; and there was." He is God eternal; he was there before the beginning and is there beyond the end.

In *Pirke Avot* (*The Ethics of the Fathers*), a tractate of the Talmud, it is written that *Torah* (God's Word, Teaching, Direction) was God's instrument of creation. "Beloved are Israel in that there was given to them a precious instrument. Greater love was proved to them in that there was given to them the precious instrument whereby the world was created" (*Av.* 3:18). The great teacher Akiba makes his meaning clear by adding, "As it is said: For good doctrine I give you, forsake not my *Torah*" (see Prov. 4:2).

Believers in Yeshua remember that he came as the Word, through whom all things were made (John 1:1–3). He was God's Son and the agent of creation (Heb. 1:2). "Without him nothing made had being" (John 1:3).

Nature Proclaims God

David, the "sweet singer of Isra'el" (2 Sam. 23:1), found that nature spoke eloquently of God. For him—perhaps out at night, watching the sheep—the heavens, moon, and stars proclaimed God's greatness. He marveled that such a God could take note of ordinary human beings. The thought stimulated him to an exclamation of praise: "ADONAI! Our Lord! How glorious is your name throughout the earth!" (Ps. 8:2[1]). The green fields and quiet streams reminded him of God's gentle care. The dark ravines spoke of God's faithfulness in times of trouble (Ps. 23). On another occasion, he sensed the heavens speaking of God's grace and faithfulness, the mountains God's righteousness, and the sea God's judgment (Ps. 36:6-7[5–6]).

The writer of Psalm 93 contemplated the mighty sea breakers— perhaps the most powerful force he knew. For him, God was even mightier than the mighty ocean (v. 4).

The New Covenant (Testament) writings teach us that God is to be found in nature, even by those who have had no teaching. *Sha'ul*, in his first recorded sermon to Gentile pagans, quotes Psalm 146 in saying:

> Turn from these worthless things to the living God who made heaven and earth and the sea and everything in them! In times past, he allowed all peoples to walk in their own ways; yet he did not leave himself without evidence of his own nature; be- cause he does good things, giving you rain from heaven and crops in their seasons, filling you with food and your hearts with happiness! (Acts 14:15–17)

In his letter to the believers in Rome, he declared, "Ever since the creation of the universe his invisible qualities—both his eternal power and his divine nature—have been clearly seen, because they can be understood from what he has made" (Rom. 1:20). Even those without the written Scriptures can see something of God's nature through his creation.

The *Shulchan Aruch*, Joseph Caro's sixteenth-century codification of rabbinical Judaism, contains a poem that includes the lines:

> One who is outside at Nisan-time,
> and sees trees just beginning to bloom,
> recites the following blessing:
> Blessed are you, O Lord our God,
> Ruler of the universe,
> who has made the world so full
> it lacks nothing,
> and has created in it
> beautiful creations and beautiful trees
> for human beings to enjoy. (*Orach Chaim* 226:1)

I found Caro's words in a leaflet entitled "Blessings and Prayers." The leaflet also contained an anonymous poem describing the sometimes less than gentle effects of nature.

Praised be the Lord
of imperfection.
His flaws are everywhere:
In the elm's unbalanced foliage
and the asymmetric faces of his creatures.
He forms the ripping floods
that tear the forests
and bends tornadoes in a twisting dance.
The lion is blotched with age and mud,
and the Shabbas silverware lies stained
as a reminder.
Praised be his Torah of scratches and scars.
Praised be his discolorations
for they are puzzles and poems
of his sacred character.

My Personal Experience

The English have a saying: "You are nearer God's heart in a garden than anywhere else on earth." I have not found this the case. When I first became a believer in Yeshua, I was a student at a college on the south coast of England. That first year, I used to take every opportunity to walk along the beach, soaking up the awesome creative power of God, as seen in the sea in all its moods. Ever since, I have found it easier to worship him by the sea than anywhere else.

A friend invited me to stay with her at the seaside immediately after my husband died. One day she drove me to Portland Bill, a rugged promontory, leaving me to walk alone. The sea was rough; the waves were foam-flecked. The waters were crashing against the rocks. What I saw and heard perfectly expressed the tempestuousness of my grief. I could not express it for myself, because to do so would not have been acceptable to the people around me. God himself was ministering release and healing through his creation. "Bless ADONAI, my soul! . . . He heals all your diseases" (Ps. 103:1, 3).

Yeshua and Nature

Surely, Yeshua blessed God, giving thanks for his manifestations in nature—his power, his "otherness," his protection, his trustworthiness. For Yeshua, the sight of a field of beautiful flowers was a reminder of how much more our heavenly Father cares for his children (Matt. 6:28–30). The fertile vineyards—already a picture of God's people, Israel—illustrated the intertwined relationships among the Father, Yeshua the Son, and the believers in Yeshua (John 15:1–10). His ability to control the sea—that great sea, beyond the command of people—demonstrated who he was. He was God in human form.

For Thought

The earth is ADONAI's, with all that is in it,
the world and those who live there. (Ps. 24:1)

The heavens declare the glory of God,
the dome of the sky speaks the work of his hands. (Ps. 19:2[1])

Surely, the mind that conceived and designed all the wonders of creation is beyond my comprehension. How can I not submit and yield my life to him in every detail? However chaotic the world may seem, God has not lost his grip on the situation. His plan is still unfolding.

A Prayer

"Sovereign God of all creation . . . your greatness and goodness fill the universe . . . splendid are the stars which you, our God, have made! You formed them with knowledge, and fashioned them with wisdom. . . . You called to the sun, and it blazed forth light; you looked to the moon, and it circled the earth. All the hosts of heaven proclaim your praise!" (*Siddur Lev Chadash* 163).

Blessed are you, O Lord our God, King of the universe, whose might and power fill the world!

Chapter 9

Who Has Created Joy and Gladness

—

אשר ברא ששון ושמחה
Asher Bara Sasson v'Simchah

—

It has been said that no other language possesses as many words for joy as Hebrew. Simchah, sasson, *hedvah, gil, rinnah*—all these express the feeling of gladness and rejoicing that is characteristic of Judaism. God himself is a God of joy who desires to rejoice in his works (Ps. 104:31). He invites his people to rejoice before him (Deut. 12:12). Indeed, the Bratzlaver said, "God dislikes melancholy and depressed spirits" (Newman 204).

In spite of their long history of suffering and persecution, the Jewish people have remained hopeful. That sense of hope pervades the Scriptures as well as the traditions, literature, prayers, and worldview of the Jewish people. Though today some may say they have no faith in God, Judaism embodies belief in a God who will bring to pass the final triumph of justice and truth.

Our incentive to rejoice is the character of God and his works, and our rejoicing is to be *before him*. It is an obligation, not an emotion based on our current circumstances or feelings. *Torah* tells us, "You are to . . . rejoice before the LORD your God" (Lev. 23:40 NIV). The *Siddur Lev Chadash* states, "Even in the darkest times . . . we have responded to the divine command: You shall rejoice before the Eternal One your God" (349). Joy is fundamental to Judaism.

Joy in *Torah*

The Scriptures not only encourage rejoicing but are themselves the source of joy (Ps. 19:9[8]). That is the reasoning behind the rejoicing at *Shavu'ot*, the festival that traditionally commemorates the giving of

Torah on Sinai. Whatever else the Jewish people lack, they can still rejoice that God privileged them to be the trustees of *Torah*. God intended *Torah* to be a source of joy—not a straitjacket—to the otherwise poor and deprived. Hirsch points to Bereshit 60b when he states,

> To drink and to give to drink joyfully from the fountain of the Torah even if thousands scorn it; to cultivate joyfully the light of the Torah, even if thousands announce its extinction; to know that God, from Whom the fountain wells forth, will cause it to flow on pure, that He Who kindled the light will never allow it to become extinguished. This leads to שמחה [*simchah*] in God. (88)

This note of joy in *Torah* is particularly noticeable in the Hasidic movement, where the emphasis has been on spontaneity and ebullient worship. The Bratzlaver taught that "joy is attained through Torah and Worship" (Newman 204).

Because *Torah* and joy are inseparable, Israel received *Torah* with joy. Likewise, we should read God's Word joyfully, obeying it in the same spirit. It follows that the public reading of *Torah* should be a joyful exercise. Therefore, a mourner does not exercise the privilege, neither does he recite Talmud. The traditional view is that God gave Talmud on Sinai and that Talmud as well as *Torah* is Israel's joy.

The culminating expression of this joy in *Torah* is Simchat Torah, the day of the Rejoicing of the Law, at the end of Sukkot (the Feast of Tabernacles). On this day, the scrolls are carried in a processional around the synagogue to the accompaniment of much rejoicing and sometimes dancing. What a treasure God entrusted to Israel! Why should we not rejoice? Surely, Christians can rejoice too—that God preserved his *Torah* by means of his people Israel. *Torah* is a lamp to our feet and a light to our path (Ps. 119:105).

Joy in Doing Good Deeds

A *mitzvah* is a command, a sacred duty, a good deed. The Jewish sages coined the term *simchah shel mitzvah*. It describes the joy with which one should perform a *mitzvah* and the joy that follows from the good performance of that sacred duty. Righteousness is not just the performance of the commands of *Torah* but the manner of that performance—not grudgingly, as of necessity, but willingly, with joy. Because God himself takes joy in *Torah*, this kind of obedience brings joy to God's heart. One of the shorter tractates of the Talmud deals with appropriate behavior for a scholar. In it we find these words: "If you have fulfilled my words with joy, my servants will come to greet you, and I myself will go forth to meet you, and say to you, 'May your coming be in peace' " (*Derekh Eretz Zuta* 4:6). As God's servants seek to be like God, what delights his heart will delight their hearts too.

Joy must accompany the performance of any religious deed for that deed to have value, whether it be *Torah* study, prayer, an act of charity, or a kindness. "Great heartfelt joy is indispensable." So taught Isaac Luria in the sixteenth century (Fine 71). This does not mean a lighthearted, irreverent approach to God. Joy must be the outcome of sincerity and devotion. "One should not stand up to pray in a mood of sadness, idleness, jocularity, small talk, levity, or idle chatter, but in a mood of joy in the doing of God's will" (*Siddur Lev Chadash* 350).

Moses Hayim Luzzatto, writing in the eighteenth century, taught that the wellspring of such joy in service is a sense of privilege and wonder. It is amazing that God has chosen and permitted us to love and to serve him, the incomparable One (568). God is infinite; we are insignificant. However, the more we experience this joy, the more we grow in spiritual stature (Ginsburgh 242). The joy of our service demonstrates the strength of our faith in, and the depth of our love for, God. A miserable believer makes an unconvincing witness.

One of the Hasidic rabbis, the Alexanderer, underlined this point by citing Deuteronomy 28. Here, Moses lists a series of curses and then remarks that the people were susceptible to these curses "because you didn't serve ADONAI your God with joy and gladness in your heart" (v. 47). That, said the Alexanderer, is how important it is always to be full of joy (Newman 202).

Joy in Worship

Perhaps joy in worship begins with thanksgiving for all that God has done for us, all that he has provided. Sometimes we offer the thanksgiving in anticipation (Ps. 104:34), sometimes in retrospect (1 Sam. 2:1). One day God will make everything right. Then we will be able to express gratitude freely, in gladness and with rejoicing (Joel 2:23).

In the meantime, we worship God for who and what he is, rejoicing in his unchanging nature. Psalm 100 gives vibrant expression to such joy in worship. The psalms of praise have an important place in synagogue worship. There is a story of another Hasid, the Maggid, who was in desperately poor health. When he recited the verse "Sing unto the Lord a new song," his weakness would leave him and he would sing with uninhibited joy like a little child (Jacobs, *Hasidic Prayer* 95). Joy is one of the great essentials in the worship of God, along with love, awe, and devotion. God desires that we come into his presence with joy (Isa. 56:7). We are in communion with Almighty God. That is cause for great rejoicing.

Prayer involves more than coming to God with a list of requests. The rabbis taught that it should be a joyful act. Perhaps the greatest achievement of the Hasidic movement was to restore a sense of joy to the prayer life of ordinary Jewish people. The Hasidim believe that one should offer prayer "in a spirit of boundless joy, delight, and warmth" (Jacobs, *Hasidic Prayer* 93). The Besht went even further, teaching that joyless prayers would not be effective: "No child can be born except through pleasure and joy. By the same token, if one wishes his prayers to bear fruit, he must offer them with pleasure and with joy" (Newman 203).

Joy in God's Presence

"In your presence is unbounded joy," proclaimed the psalmist (Ps. 16:11). *The Siddur Lev Chadash* expresses a development of this thought: "There is no sadness in the presence of the Holy One" (351). The *Sh'khinah* (God's glory) is believed to rest upon people when they experience the joy of *Simchah shel Mitzvah* (*Shab.* 30b). Therefore, it follows that the *Sh'khinah* will not dwell in a person whose spirit is without joy. Likewise, the Talmud states that the *Ruach haKodesh* will rest only on one whose heart is joyful (*Sukkah* 5:1).

Joy in Celebration

God gave us Sabbaths and festivals as occasions of rejoicing. "If you call *Shabbat* a delight . . . ," promises the Lord, "I will make you ride on the heights" (Isa. 58:13–14). Shabbat, rightly observed, is the true joy of the Jewish home—a weekly oasis in what can seem like a desert. Two things in particular give expression to that joy. The candles that are lit as the Sabbath arrives shed light upon the table, just as God sheds joy over the home. The *kiddush* (sanctification) cup of wine symbolizes our joy as we celebrate this day that has meant so much to the Jewish people. It is the memorial of creation and of redemption. It is also the reminder of Israel's calling to be different, a people holy unto God. The rabbis say there is no rejoicing without wine.

Weddings are special times of rejoicing and are celebrated with not just one but seven blessings—the *Sheva B'rakhot*. We bless the Lord for creation and for the special relationship between male and female. We remember Jerusalem and pray that she may "rejoice through her children." We should never think of our personal happiness above that of Jerusalem. Only the last two blessings focus on the couple, praying that they may have joy in their union. The seventh blessing goes like this:

> Blessed are you, O Lord our God, King of the universe, who created joy and gladness, groom and bride, mirth and song, pleasure and delight, love, brotherhood, peace and companionship. May there soon be heard in the cities of Judah and in the streets of Jerusalem the sound of joy and happiness, the sound of groom and the sound of bride, the jubilant sound of bridegrooms from their canopies and of youths from their feasts of song. Blessed are you, Lord, who causes the groom to rejoice with the bride.

Joy in Community

Every festival is to be "invested with the character of joy" (*Pes.* 109a). Each *Yom Tov* (festival day) brings its particular way of expressing the joy of living before God. We may be remembering a past deliverance or celebrating a gathered harvest. Perhaps we are giving thanks for a special provision of God to his people in the past. A vital component of this festival joy is the sense of community. Individual joy is not enough. We prepare food for one another. We wear our finest clothes. We attend celebrations that revolve around the festival. The call is to submerge our individual feelings of sadness in order that we may share in the joy of being part of a community (Hirsch 211). The Talmud states that God specifically gave these days to Israel to be times of remembering and of joy (*Ber.* 49a). Indeed, the festival "peace offerings" were also *Shalmei Simchah* (Peace Offerings of Joy).

Sukkot is the most joyous of festivals. The water pouring ceremony of Temple times became quite exuberant. One rabbi stated, "He who has not seen the rejoicing of the water-drawing ceremony has never seen rejoicing in his life" (*Sukk.* 5:1). Everyone is invited to share in the joy of this festival. The prophet Zechariah foresaw a time when not only Israel but those from many nations as well would share the joy of *Sukkot* (Zech. 14:16).

Joy in Fasts

Even the fasts were to be occasions for joy. The Hasidic teachers believed that, though repentance may come with humbling, sorrow, and tears, its outcome is joyful. If that repentance is wholehearted and genuine, God will respond with forgiveness (Newman 376). This was in keeping with the talmudic tradition that one should observe Yom Kippur (the Day of Atonement) with great joy "because it is a day of forgiveness and pardon" (*Ta'anith* 30b). To be sure, the fact that one's name is written in the Book of Life is a greater cause for rejoicing than anything else. It is this assurance that is so precious to those who follow Yeshua as Messiah. "Don't be glad that the spirits submit to you," he advised his followers after a successful time of ministry; "be glad that your names have been recorded in heaven" (Luke 10:20). Hence, in a sense, Yom Kippur is a festival as well as a fast.

Some fasts are memorials of Israel's historical tragedies. Zechariah told of a day when even these occasions would be "times of joy, gladness and cheer for the house of Y'hudah [Judah]" (Zech. 8:19). This may seem inconceivable to us now, caught up as we are in Israel's suffering. However, one day God will enter history again with triumph to establish righteousness. Then we will remember what *he* has done more than what *they* did. In the same way, at Passover, we remember God's redemptive act more than Pharaoh's cruelty. This is not to belittle the suffering of the Jewish people but rather to emphasize God's miracles, wonders, and power to deliver us from our enemies.

Joy in Dark Times

Judaism is essentially a realistic faith. The *Siddur Lev Chadash* acknowledges that "it is not easy to rejoice when we carry within ourselves a private burden of pain or sorrow or frustration, or when we remember the sufferings of humanity" (349). However, we are always aware that mourning will one day be turned into joy. The desert will rejoice. In the face of bereavement, we affirm God's sovereignty in the words of the *Kaddish*:

> Blessed, praised and glorified, exalted, extolled and honored, magnified and lauded be the name of the Holy One, blessed be he; though he be high above all the blessings and hymns, praises, and consolations, which are uttered in the world; and say ye, Amen.

God promised, "I will turn their mourning into joy, comfort and gladden them after their sorrow" (Jer. 31:12[13]). Even regarding the loss of the Temple, the embodiment of all Israel's national disasters, grief should be mixed with joy. The Lord is with us in exile, still present among us (Newman 284). The talmudist Nachmanides, known as the

Ramban (1194–1270), put it this way: "The loss of all else which delighted my eyes is compensated by my present joy in a day passed within your courts, O Jerusalem . . . I weep bitterly (over your ruins) but I find joy in my heart" (*Encyclopedia of Judaism*). Pain is never the last word in God's book.

The Hasidim majored on joy: in worship, in community, in living. They believed that, while sadness is not innately sinful, it can lead to a hardening of the heart, which *is* sinful. It also spoils personal relationships and bars the way to ecstasy in worship (Newman 91, 243–44).

Joy in Religious Experience and All of Life

All branches of Judaism have taught that genuine spirituality reveals itself in joy. Nehemiah taught his contemporaries that joy in the Lord would be a source of strength to them in their difficult situation (Neh. 8:10). The Baal Shem Tov claimed that the joy we feel in cleaving to God is the measure of our righteousness (Newman 134). In the *Siddur Lev Chadash* of the London Union of Liberal and Progressive Synagogues, we find this statement: "Joy is a religious feeling, appropriate to religious observance and conducive to religious experience" (350).

Because there is no separation between the physical and the spiritual, joy spills over into every area of life. Jewish people are characteristically optimistic, seeking occasions for rejoicing and celebration. Joy must be healthy, without triumphalism. At the Passover *seder,* we remove wine from the cup in memory of the Egyptians who died. Our celebrations do not, as a rule, degenerate into drunkenness or licentiousness. The ideal is a joy based on inner security, not dependent on physical circumstances.

It seems that one rabbi did not have much in worldly assets.

. . . he was impoverished and suffered much throughout his life. But his sublime faith in *HaShem* [the Name] was such that he viewed his life as wholly within the hands of *HaShem*. His dependence was total. In that context, a serenity and wellspring of *simchah* (gladness) pervaded his entire life. (Forst 24)

Joy in Salvation

Habakkuk wrote at a time when national disaster loomed, but he triumphantly affirmed, "I will take joy in the God of my salvation" (3:18). Likewise, Isaiah promised, "You will joyfully draw water from the springs of salvation" (12:3). These words remind us of *Sukkot*. In the synagogue, we pray for rain during this festival. We also recall the water pouring ceremony at the Temple. On each day of *Sukkot*, a priest would take a golden pitcher filled with water from the Pool of Siloam, carry it to the Temple, and pour it on the altar as an offering to God. Surely Yeshua was referring to this ceremony when, in the Temple courts at *Sukkot*, he cried, "If anyone is thirsty, let him keep coming to me and drinking! Whoever puts his trust in me, as the Scripture says, rivers of living water will flow from his inmost being!" (John 7:37–38). Perhaps, he was making a play on the word "salvation"—the meaning of his own name, Yeshua. Yeshua was offering real joy, not based on hope but on assurance, the certainty of salvation.

For Thought

The natural optimism of the Jewish people has been strained almost beyond bearing during the past century. People need something more than optimism to sustain joy, and that something is certainty. It is not enough to hope that tomorrow may be better than today, since history tells us that suffering may well lie ahead for us. However, Yeshua said, "You will grieve, but your grief will turn to joy. . . . I am going to see you again. Then your hearts will be full of joy, and no one will take your joy away from you" (John 16:20, 22). He made a promise we know he will fulfill, because it rests on the surety of his Resurrection. I once heard someone say to my husband, "Your Jewishness is obviously very precious to you. What do you have now that was lacking before you believed in Jesus?" The answer came immediately, and in one word—"Assurance." Our joy takes root in the historical fact of the Resurrection of Yeshua the Messiah. Therefore, it can never be taken from us. Hallelujah!

"Rejoice in union with the Lord always! I will say it again: rejoice!" (Phil. 4:4).

> Even if the fig tree doesn't blossom,
> and no fruit is on the vines,
> even if the olive tree fails to produce,
> and the fields yield no food at all,
> even if the sheep vanish from the sheep pen,
> and there are no cows in the stalls;
> still, I will rejoice in *Adonai*,
> I will take joy in the God of my salvation. (Hab. 3:17–18)

A Prayer

Lord, the source of joy, discipline my heart to be open to you. I want to let you in to share my pain, my sadness, my frustration, and my failure. Then you will share with me your joy.

Help me, O Lord, continually to draw water from the wells of salvation, and to share that water with those I meet today.

Blessed are you, O Lord, who has created joy and gladness.

Chapter 10

Who Has Brought Us to This Season

—

שהחיינו וקימנו והגיענו לזמן הזה
*Shehekhiyanu v'Kiyamanu v'Higiyanu
Laz'man HaZeh*

—

What sculptors do with stone, writers with words, painters with pigments, and musicians with notes," says Jonathan Sacks, "Judaism does with deeds . . . the Sabbath . . . on Passover . . . in the dozens of blessings we have for the varied pleasures of the senses, recapturing the wonder that we are here at all to enjoy this world that might not have been. ("Credo")

For me, the most precious of these many blessings of which the British Chief Rabbi speaks is the *Shehekhiyanu*: "*Barukh atah Adonai Eloheynu, Melekh ha'olam, shehekhiyanu v'kiyamanu v'higiyanu laz'man hazeh*" ("Blessed are you, O Lord our God, King of the universe, who has kept us alive and sustained us and brought us to this season"). Here, we have the opportunity to recapture the wonder that we are still here to enjoy God's world. We can give expression to our delight in the rhythmic nature of God's goodness and provision. He gives us much more than what is merely necessary for survival. In the *Shehekhiyanu*, we tell God of the delight we feel in receiving his bountiful gifts.

Wonder, Rejoice, and Bless

Every country has its seasonal delights. In England, where I write, there are few that do not look for the first snowdrops, the delicate white flowers that are the first to bloom at the end of winter, as January draws to its close. Only last week, the first snow-drops opened in my garden. There may be snow tomorrow, as the forecasters have promised—but spring *will* come. For this annual sign of hope I lift my face to heaven and make the *Shehekhiyanu*. I will do so again when I see the first butterfly-drawing flowers on the buddleia in mid-summer. The morning I wrote the first draft of this chapter, I stood in my garden and saw the first peacock butterfly of the season on my neighbor's buddleia. Again, I said the familiar words "*Barukh atah Adonai.*" It may happen each July, but it still takes my breath away.

What beautiful creatures God has made! What a privilege it is that I am still here to enjoy them!

The reddening pyracantha berries in the autumn will stimulate the same response. This sense of delight is not only for the crazy garden-loving English. I remember gasping with wonder the first time I saw the glorious colors of the American fall. Many of you will identify with my joy in these experiences. Is it not a privilege to have a ready-made blessing to express our appreciation to the Maker and Giver of these good things!

Have you ever planted a fruit tree or bush, then waited and watched for those precious first fruits? You pick them, perhaps only two or three that first year. The occasion cannot pass uncelebrated: "Blessed are you, O Lord our God, King of the universe, who has kept us alive and sustained us and brought us to this season." Indeed, this is a multipurpose *b'rakhah*, one that is appropriate for many special occasions.

According to the Talmud, it is appropriate to make this *b'rakhah* when we have built a new house or purchased new cooking vessels or clothes (*Ber.* 54a; 59b). We may use it to express joy at seeing a friend after a separation of thirty days (*Ber.* 58b). We should only do that, however, if the joy of reunion is genuine and the friend a good one! This is a *b'rakhah* of delight, not of duty.

When my high school class met for our fortieth reunion, they invited me to "say grace" before the meal. I thought it was fitting to recite the *Shehekhiyanu*, having first explained its derivation. My classmates agreed that it was appropriate. They even gave me the same privilege ten years later!

Seasonal Delights

The *Shehekhiyanu* reminds us that we see God's hand in bringing us to every new season and every special event. It is a "prayer of gratitude and celebration recited at the arrival of a holiday, or when something is experienced for the first time during a Jewish year (e.g. new fruit eaten, a new garment worn, a major accomplishment made)" (Ross 321). We recite it on the first night of every festival (*Pes.* 102b) and on the eighth night of *Sukkot.* We may also say it when building our *sukkah* (*Pes.* 7b) and making our *lulav* (*Sukk.* 46a). The *sukkah* is the open-air shelter used during the festival as a reminder of the desert wanderings. The *lulav* is a bound bunch of willow, palm, and myrtle branches. It is used, together with a citron, in synagogue worship at this season. *The Rabbinic Anthology* says of the *Shehekhiyanu* that it is "a blessing in constant use on festivals and all joyous occasions" (377).

Hirsch commends the making of this *b'rakhah* "when fortunate circumstances of any kind fall to your lot, . . . events recurring from time to time, by which the preservation of the life granted to you for a time by God's love is brought to your consciousness. Thus, on tasting any new fruit for the first time in the season . . . and on the observance of a duty that recurs only once yearly . . . God is recognized as the Giver of the benefit . . . and as the Preserver of life. You dedicate yourself to Him to the fulfillment of His will in good and bad fortune as long as He preserves your life" (532).

Special Occasions

Did the returning exiles pause to utter these words, or something similar to them, when they first set foot on their own land after those seventy long years? God had kept them alive, sustaining them during the years of exile and the dangers and privations of the journey. God had brought them to this time and place, about which they and their fathers had dreamed. Surely, their spontaneous response would have been "Blessed are you, O Lord our God, King of the universe, who has kept us alive and sustained us and brought us to this season."

The *tzaddik Shim'on* (Simeon, the righteous man) knew, by revelation, that before he died he would see the Messiah. The day came when he at last held the child in his arms, and he "made a *b'rakhah* to God" (Luke 2:28). What *b'rakhah* did he make? Could it have been the *Shehekhiyanu*? What could have been more appropriate?

Yeshua would have said this blessing every time he celebrated the Passover. He would surely have learned to say it from his childhood as he helped to build the *sukkah* and make the *lulav* each fall. Did he hear it spoken as the family prepared to light the first of the Hanukkah lamps? When he became an itinerant rabbi, he must have made this *b'rakhah* many times as he passed familiar landmarks, noticing signs of the changing seasons. On many other occasions as well these words must have been on his lips.

How would *Sha'ul* have expressed himself when a longed-for visitor came to him in prison? What words came to his lips when he heard news of the spiritual growth of his "children"? What did he exclaim when he saw the believers coming to meet him as he entered Rome as a prisoner? Might it not have been with the words of the *Shehekhiyanu*?

For Thought

"Who has kept us alive": These days, we take longevity for granted. Indeed, our lives sometimes seem to be too long. We may feel that our life is a burden rather than a blessing. I have had more than the allotted three score years and ten. I constantly need to remind myself to keep my eyes open for opportunities to bless the Lord for the life he gives me. I should bless him for eyes to see and ears to hear, for friendships, and for preserving me to enjoy my grandchildren. He is the keeping God.

"Who has sustained us": Whenever another year has passed since I last said the *Shehekhiyanu* for an annual event, a glance back is appropriate. How often has God come alongside me to share my burden, to ease my way? I may have fallen, but he picked me up and set me on my feet again. I may have failed, but he gave me another chance. I may have experienced great pain, but he did not leave me to bear it alone. Each pain has left me better equipped for ministry. He is the sustaining God.

"Who has brought us to this season": The past is now behind me. Today is the door to another season, and I must go through it. I may have suffered bereavement since last making the *b'rakhah* for a particular event, and it is difficult to say the words. I would rather stand still in time and stay with the loved one I have lost. However, for the child of God this is not an option. Today is here for living. Tomorrow calls. We have to keep moving forward with our Messiah. The goal is to leave the past behind, straining forward to what lies ahead (Phil. 3:13–14). The Lord has brought me to this season. I can trust him with my future.

A Prayer

> *I give you thanks with all my heart. . . .*
> *When I called, you answered me,*
> *you made me bold and strong. . . .*

You keep me alive when surrounded by danger;
you put out your hand when my enemies rage;
with your right hand you save me.
ADONAI will fulfill his purpose for me.
Your grace, ADONAI, continues forever.
Don't abandon the work of your hands! (Ps. 138:1, 3, 7–8)

Thank you Lord, for the blessings you shower upon me, always more than I ask or can imagine. Give me, I pray, the grace of open eyes. Enable me to see you in the day-to-day events of life. Soften my heart that I may step into the unseen future with my hand in yours.

Blessed are you, O Lord our God, who has kept us alive and sustained us and brought us to this season.

Chapter 11

Who Remembers His Covenant

—

זוכר הברית ונאמן בבריתו וקים באמרו

Zokher HaB'rit v'Ne'eman biB'rito
v'Kayam b'Ma'amaro

—

The sky is overcast, purple-black. The rain pours down determinedly. What a day! Now turn around. Look behind and you may see one of nature's great performances. A flawless, seven-colored double arch straddles the somber sky. How can you not respond, "Blessed are you, O Lord our God, King of the universe, who remembers his covenant, is faithful to his covenant, and fulfills his word" (*Ber.* 59a)?

A Covenant God

The rainbow is the God-given sign of the *b'rit* (covenant) that God made with Noah after the Flood (Gen. 9:13), promising that he would never again destroy all life in this way. "When I look at it," said God, "I will remember the everlasting covenant between myself and every living creature on the earth." It is we—not God—who need the reminder that God is faithful and true to what he has promised. We see the rainbow and we make the *b'rakhah*, affirming not only the covenant that God made with Noah but also those that followed as God's plan unfolded.

By the terms of the Abrahamic *b'rit* (Gen. 17:7–14), God promised the land and the blessing and instituted circumcision as the first covenant sign. The deliverance of Israel from Egypt was a covenant act, leading to Sinai (Exod. 24:4–8). There the *Torah* was given and accepted and God confirmed Shabbat as the second covenant sign

(Exod. 31:13–17): "Blessed is he who gave Sabbath for rest to his people Israel in love, for a sign and a covenant" (*Ber.* 49a). Covenant is also identified as *Torah*—"the words of the covenant" (*Makk.* 22b). Repeatedly, God enjoins Israel to obey the words of the covenant.

The concept of *b'rit* is basic to the Scriptures and to Judaism. Circumcision, Shabbat, and *Torah* are the building blocks, but *b'rit* is the foundation stone. "The only true principle of the Jewish faith is that God has made a covenant with his people" (Jacobs, *Theology* 351).

Traditionally, salt has been associated with *b'rit* (Lev. 2:13) and should therefore always be on the Shabbat and festival table as a reminder. The Talmud states that covenant status may involve suffering. The declaration "these are the words of the covenant" (Deut. 28:69[29:1]) come at the end of a chapter cataloging the sufferings of Israel to come (*Ber.* 5a).

We remember the everlasting covenant of peace promised in the book of Ezekiel (37:26), with its guarantee of inner transformation. Jeremiah spoke of a New Covenant (31:30–33[31–34]) in which God will write his *Torah* on our hearts and all will know the Lord. At that time all sins will be forgiven—and forgotten—by God.

All these covenants assumed and affirmed a relationship. "I will take you as my people, and I will be your God" (Exod. 6:7). "I will be their God, and they will be my people" (Jer. 31:32). The relationship is mutual; it rests primarily on God's choice, not ours. However, we may enjoy that relationship only as we respond to God.

The concept of *b'rit* is one of the most exciting themes running through the *Tanakh* because of what it tells us about the nature of God. Although he is unique, almighty, holy—totally "other"—he is also social. God wishes to live, not in glorious isolation, but in company, in relationship. His plan is to dwell among his people (Exod. 25:8).

The Remembering God

The only thing God is ever going to forget is his people's sins (Jer. 31:33[34]). He will never forget his people: "Can a woman forget her child at the breast . . . ? Even if these were to forget, I would not forget you" (Isa. 49:15). He will never forget his words, his promises, or his covenant. In the dark days of slavery in Egypt, this is the message with which he first came to Moses: "I have remembered my covenant" (Exod. 6:5). Through all the succeeding generations, we see God remembering his covenant, always mindful of his people, still wanting to live among them.

At the end of his life, Moses proclaimed the faithfulness of God:

I will proclaim the name of ADONAI.
Come, declare the greatness of our God!
The Rock! His work is perfect,
for all his ways are just.
A trustworthy God who does no wrong,
he is righteous and straight. (Deut. 32:3–4)

Our God is indeed "God, the faithful God, who keeps his covenant" (Deut. 7:9). Hirsch tells us that, when things look bad for Israel in today's world, we should look back to those post-Exodus days. "Learn how God sustained your forefathers in their early wanderings in the wilderness. He is with you in your present wandering in the wilderness too" (126). The response to God's faithfulness, says Hirsch again, has to be trust. "*Emunah*, trust in God, means to hold fast to God, to His promise, to His law, to His grace, even though His ruling hand does not show itself in our experience and the fulfilment of His promises seems to lie far away" (30).

The Trustworthy God

God will always keep his word—not just his covenant promises but all his other promises as well. For Israel this means that he will never abandon us, because that would be against his nature. "I am God, not a human being," he says to faithless Israel (Hos. 11:9). As long as the laws of nature are in force, Israel will continue to be "a nation in my presence forever" (Jer. 31:35[36]). Today, surrounding hostile nations threaten; the enemy within the Land burns with hatred; anti-Semitism is again on the increase worldwide. Nevertheless, God has made eternal promises to his people Israel, and he is trustworthy.

There are implications here for believers. God will always be faithful to what he has promised, although we may be confused about what these promises are. To base our faith on promises not found in Scripture is to build a house on sand. That way leads to disappointment and disillusionment. God has not promised ease or immunity against the common afflictions of life. A promise given on my wedding day has remained with me ever since: "Delight yourself in ADONAI, and he will give you your heart's desire" (Ps. 37:4). Think about that! He will give me my heart's desire if my heart's desire is for him. When trouble comes, the words of the twenty-third psalm still apply today:

> Even if I pass through death-dark ravines,
> I will fear no disaster; for you are with me. (Ps. 23:4)

Yeshua as the Fulfillment of the New Covenant

According to a traditional story, Abraham feared that his covenant would be superseded because of the inevitable failure of his descendants. Then God said to him, "When thy children fall into sin and evil deeds, I will arrange for a righteous man who will cause the balance to sink in their favor, for he will be able to say to the attribute of justice, 'Enough, I will take *him*, and I will make him atone for *them*'" (Montefiore and Loewe 229).

At his last Passover *seder*, Yeshua claimed to be the fulfillment of the New Covenant. Covenants were always sealed with blood, and so it would be with him. As we drink the third cup—the cup of redemption—we recall his words: "This is my blood, which ratifies the New Covenant, my blood shed on behalf of many, so that they may have their sins forgiven" (Matt. 26:28). This is the ultimate affirmation of our relationship with God. If he sacrificed his only Son for us, he must really love us.

One day, at the end of time, our relationship with God will be complete and perfect: "See! God's *Sh'khinah* is with mankind, and he will live with them. They will be his people, and he himself, God-with-them, will be their God" (Rev. 21:3). Then we will really know him. Then sin will totally—finally—lose its grip on us.

For Thought

Life may be hard and bewildering for you just now. You may be tempted to give up hope and wallow in despair or self-pity. Look back. Has not God has always been faithful in the past—in history and in your personal experience? He is the unchanging One. Look up. See the rainbow, and bless the God who will not fail you now.

He has said that nothing can separate you from "the love of God which comes to us through the Messiah Yeshua" (Rom. 8:39). He has promised that no one can snatch you from his hand (John 10:28). He has declared that he will never abandon you (Heb. 13:5). He gives the assurance that one day you will be with him forever (John 14:3). He remembers. He is faithful.

We can trust him. He is the God who speaks to us with his mouth and fulfills his promises with his hand (2 Chron. 6:4).

A Prayer

Lord, my life does not seem to make sense these days. I do not know how I got into this situation. I have no idea how to handle it. Then your rainbow appears, not every time I am in despair, but often when I need to see it most. It reminds me of your faithfulness. You have promised that nothing can separate me from your love, and I believe you.

Blessed are you, O Lord our God, King of the universe, who never forgets his people and is faithful to his New Covenant, fulfilled in Yeshua.

Bless the Lord
in the Congregation

Chapter 12

The *Amidah*

—

עמידה

Amidah

—

The centerpiece of Jewish corporate prayer life is the *Amidah* (Standing Prayer). It is also known as the *Shemoneh Esreh* (Eighteen Blessings)— so called because it originally consisted of eighteen *b'rakhot*. Later the rabbis added another. One stands to say the *Amidah*. It is also simply referred to as the *Tefillah* (the Prayer) because it is the "prayer par excellence" (Friedlander 437). Next to the *Sh'ma*, these *b'rakhot* are the most important part of the synagogue services. They consist of praise of God's goodness, various petitions to God, and an expression of thanksgiving to God.

Concerning "the blessing that Moshe, the man of God, spoke over the people of Isra'el before his death" (Deut. 33:1), the Talmud says,

> Moses did not begin with Israel's needs, until he had opened with God's praise. He was like an orator, standing by the judge's seat, who was hired by a client to plead for him. But before speaking of the client's needs, the orator opened with the praises of the king, saying, "Happy is the world by reason of his rule, by reason of his justice": all the people joined in the praise. Then he opened his client's case; he ended, too, with praise of the king. So did Moses. So, too, did David and Solomon. So, too, did the Elders who composed the Eighteen Benedictions for Israel to use in prayer. They did not open with Israel's needs, but with, "The great, mighty, and awful God ... Holy art thou and awful is thy name." Only then came, "Thou loosest the bound, and healest the sick." Finally they ended with, "We give thee thanks." (qtd. in Montefiore and Loewe 357)

The *Amidah* is a part of public worship, but it is read silently by all before being repeated aloud by the one who is leading prayers. This gives it a private and personal as well as a communal dimension. Rabban Gamaliel maintained that "a person should recite the *Shemoneh Esrei* prayer every day" (*Ber.* 4:3). The spirit behind this frequent recitation is that of dedication to God. There is an ongoing reaching out to God, a yearning to have communion with him, allied to a desire to strive after the godly life. Hirsch described it as "a direct example of striving sanctified by the idea of God" (492). The late British Chief Rabbi Hertz put it this way: "These oldest congregational prayers of Judaism satisfy the cravings of a pious heart for communion with God, and give expression to praise, thanksgiving, confession, and petition" (*ADP* 130).

The Structure of the *Amidah*

The *Amidah* has three sections. The first three *b'rakhot* are expressions of praise to God. They glorify him for his "everlasting love, eternal might, and infinite holiness" (*ADP* 130). In recognizing God for who he is and what he has done, we express our trust in him and our desire to respond to him, by dedicating ourselves to his service (Hirsch 482). Our relationship with God finds its security in *his* person, *his* deeds. This reflects the pattern of the Ten Words (Ten Commandments). They open with "I am ADONAI your God, who brought you out of the land of Egypt, out of the abode of slavery" (Exod. 20:2).

The twelve (now thirteen) intermediate *b'rakhot* are various petitions—for individual, and then for national, well being, both spiritual and material. They deal with repentance, forgiveness, and healing. They plead for deliverance from trouble and for prosperity. There is also a cry for the "Ingathering of the Dispersed" (Donin 88). In these prayers, we place our future—individual and corporate—into God's hands. It is characteristic of Judaism that there is no great divide between the sacred and the secular areas of our life. We do not concern ourselves only with our physical and social well-being. Always there is the consciousness that the Jewish people are a people of destiny. Yes, God chose this people—but for a purpose. Therefore, this people look not only to "the restoration of the external national fortune" but also to "the completion of its spiritual destiny" (Hirsch 483). As material well-being accompanies "enlightenment from above," the blessings God showers upon us may help us to fulfill his will (Hirsch 483). We know that his will for Israel is—as it has always been—that Israel may be a blessing to all peoples. God said to Abraham, "By you all the families of the earth will be blessed" (Gen. 12:3).

The twelfth *b'rakhah*—*Birkat Haminim* (Destruction of Israel's Enemies) found a place in the *Amidah* at a later date. It was a response to a perceived threat to the survival of the Jewish people. Possibly, Ezra had prescribed it in response to the actions of the hostile Samaritans. However, it fell into disuse in time. Even later, it was revived with a new opening that specifically mentioned the Sadducees. Later, at Yavneh in the second century C.E., heretical sects seemed to be a threat to the nation. This *b'rakhah* has remained in the *Amidah* because the threat of annihilation is ever present. It begins with the words "For slanderers let there be no hope, and let all wickedness instantly perish." It concludes with "Blessed art thou, Lord, who breaks the power of his enemies and subdues the malicious."

The concluding three *b'rakhot* include thanksgivings as well as a look to the future—to "the re-establishment of Divine Service in the Temple of Jerusalem" (Friedlander 438). They also mention the turning of all humanity to Israel and—through Israel—to the one true God (Hirsch 484). These concluding benedictions remind one of the Aaronic blessing (Num. 6:24–26). There is an echo of this pattern in the closing phrases of what is known as "the Lord's Prayer": "For kingship, power and glory are yours forever" (Matt. 6:13).

After the *Amidah*, we recite the last verse of Psalm 19:

May the words of my mouth
and the thoughts of my heart
be acceptable in your presence,
ADONAI, my Rock and Redeemer.

This expresses the wish that "our lips, from which prayer to God has come forth, may not be defiled by unworthy language" (Friedlander 438).

The *Amidah* in Practice

In a synagogue, people rise and silently pray the *Amidah*. Then, the reader, the worship leader, recites the *b'rakhot* aloud. This silence is after the model of Hannah, who spoke to the Lord in her heart, only her lips moving. This showed the depth of her concentration (Jacobs, *Theology* 296). Silence also provides the opportunity for private confession, petition, and meditation.

Though the recitation of the *Amidah* is not limited to synagogue worship, it should always be prayed in a respectful manner. The Talmud states that one may recite the *Sh'ma* as one walks by the way, when one carries a load, or even when one lies down. For the *Amidah*, however, one must be standing erect and set down any load one had been carrying. Indeed, the Talmud goes further, teaching that one must not stand to say the *Tefillah* even when one's mind is disturbed (*Ber.* 5:1). Offering prayers without one's full concentration is considered to be disrespectful to God.

Hirsch was quite specific about this matter of respect. "Recite the *Amidah* standing," he directed. "As a servant before God your Master, with feet together, head bowed, and eyes lowered . . . your heart should be directed towards heaven, with hands resting upon one another in tranquillity, solemnity, and respect" (553). Hirsch also noted the significance of the standing position. It is symbolic of readiness for active obedience and service.

Could Yeshua Have Known the *Shemoneh Esreh*?

These *b'rakhot* were compiled over a long period of time, but it is believed that the oldest—probably the first three—date from Second Temple times, in the fourth century B.C.E. Even the later blessings were almost certainly in use during Yeshua's lifetime. The final editing took place about the year 100 C.E., at the direction of the patriarch Gamaliel, head of Judaism in the Land (Israel).

Yeshua taught his *talmidim* (disciples) how to pray (Matt. 6:9–13), saying in effect, "Start by declaring who God is; follow this by sanctifying God's name. Only then mention your personal needs." This pattern is entirely in keeping with the *Shemoneh Esreh*. We begin by proclaiming who God is, what he is, and what he has done, before making any petitions. Truly, Yeshua was teaching his followers to pray in tune with the voice of the Jewish people.

Over the next few chapters, we will look more closely at these eighteen *b'rakhot*.

For Thought

What are my priorities as I approach prayer? Do I take time to compose myself, to recall who God is? Do I come before him with *devekut* (devotion) and respect? He is my Father, yes, but he is "in heaven." He is far above and beyond me. I do not come to him by right. I come as a privilege, by invitation, by a path that he himself has cleared. What an honor! Surely some silence, some clearing of the mind, is in order before I burst into speech.

How do I order my prayers for myself and others? Do I plunge straight into my burdens and needs? Do I follow the godly pattern of beginning with what will please God?

As I come to the end of my prayer time, I might use words like the last verse of Psalm 19. They express the desire that my thoughts, my words, and indeed my whole life might be different because I have been in communion with the Holy One, blessed be he.

My prayer priorities will reflect my life's priorities!

A Prayer

Lord, open my lips, and my mouth shall declare your praise.

> *Our Father in heaven!*
>   *May your Name be kept holy.*
> *May your Kingdom come,*
>   *your will be done on earth as in heaven.*
>
> *Give us the food we need today.*
> *Forgive us what we have done wrong,*
>   *as we too have forgiven those who have wronged us.*
> *And do not lead us into hard testing,*
>   *but keep us safe from the Evil One.*
> *For kingship, power and glory are yours forever.* (Matt. 6:9–13)

"Blessed are you, O Lord our God and God of our fathers, God of Abraham, God of Isaac, and God of Jacob, the great, mighty, and revered God, the most high God . . . O King, Helper, Savior, and Shield. Blessed are you, O Lord, the Shield of Abraham" (Amidah 1).

Chapter 13

Who Makes the Dead Live

—

מחיה המתים
M'hayeh HaMetim

—

Thy might is eternal, O Lord,
Who revives the dead,
Powerful in saving,
Who makes the wind to blow and the rain to fall,
Who sustains the living with loving kindness,
Who revives the dead with great mercy,
Who supports the falling, heals the sick, frees the captive,
And keeps faith with the dead;
Who is like Thee, Almighty, and who resembles Thee,
O King who can bring death and give life,
And can make salvation blossom forth.
And faithful art Thou to revive the dead.
Blessed art Thou, Lord, who makes the dead live. (*Amidah* 2)

Life after Death in Tradition

The second *b'rakhah* of the *Amidah* expresses belief in God the giver of life to the dead. Maimonides felt bound to enshrine a doctrine of Resurrection in his thirteenth principle: "I believe with perfect faith that there will be a Resurrection of the dead at the time when it shall please the Creator, blessed be his Name, and exalted be the remembrance of him for ever and ever." The rabbis have taught that nature itself demonstrates, through the seasonal coming of rain to bring the dead seed to life, that the Creator is a God of Resurrection (Hertz, *The Authorised Daily Prayer Book with Commentary* 133–34). He is a God we can trust for this life. We can also trust him for what lies beyond the grave. He was mighty to save in history, and he lovingly sustains us now. We can trust him to remember and to redeem "those who sleep in the dust." His protection, says Hertz, "does not cease at the portals of the grave. He is mightier than death, and in his eyes the dead have not died" (Hertz, *The Authorised Daily Prayer Book with Commentary* 133).

This particular *b'rakhah* became a test of orthodoxy. Who knew if a visiting teacher had heretical views? See if he will recite the second *b'rakhah*. The doctrine of Resurrection became an important point of division between the Pharisees and the Sadducees. A Sadducee would hesitate to proclaim, "God quickens the dead." *Sha'ul* used this division. "Brothers," he cried when standing trial before the Sanhedrin, "I myself am a *Parush* [Pharisee] and the son of *P'rushim* [Pharisees]; and it is concerning the hope of the resurrection of the dead that I am being tried!" (Acts 23:6). The Talmud states that "all of Israel shares in the future world" (*Av.* 1:1). It also says that "the righteous of all nations of the earth share in the future world" (*San.* 10:2). It goes even further. Those who deny this doctrine will not qualify for the world to come. "These are they that have no share in the world to come: he that says that no Resurrection of the dead is taught in the law" (*San.* 10:1).

Life after Death in the *Tanakh*

References to life after death occur throughout the *Tanakh*. Moses quoted God as saying, "I put to death, and I make alive" (Deut. 32:39). David cried to God in faith, "You will not abandon me to Sh'ol, you will not let your faithful one see the Abyss" (Ps. 16:10). Hosea seems to have believed that there is a life after death. "Come, let us return to Adonai. . . . After two days, he will revive us; on the third day, he will raise us up; and we will live in his presence" (Hos. 6:1–2). Daniel specifically predicted an awakening beyond the grave: "Many of those sleeping in the dust of the earth will awaken" (Dan. 12:2). Perhaps Job attained the peak of resurrection faith. From the depths of degradation and loss, he declared, "I know that my Redeemer lives . . . ; so that after my skin has been thus destroyed, then even without my flesh, I will see God. I will see him for myself" (Job 19:26–27).

As recorded in *Sanhedrin* 90b, Rabban Gamaliel (90 c.e.) cited three scriptural proofs of the Resurrection:

> The Sadducees asked Rabban Gamaliel, "How can it be proved that God will revive the dead again?" He answered: "From the Torah, from the prophets, and from the writings. From the Torah: God said to Moses, 'Behold, you are about to sleep with your fathers; then you will rise' (Deut. 31:16). From the

prophets: 'Thy dead shall live, thy bodies shall rise' (Is. 26:19). From the writings: 'May your palate be like the best wine that goes down for my lover smoothly and makes the lips of the sleepers (or: deceased) murmur' " (Song of Solomon 7:9). (Lapide 61)

Tzidduk HaDin (The Righteousness of God's Judgment)

One might think that suffering and despair would kill hope for the future. Indeed, we know that many have lost faith because of the Holocaust. However, Pinchas Lapide claims that belief in Resurrection grew out of the experience of suffering. "If God is all-just, and all-merciful, then death in this world cannot be the final end" (54). This is the tone of the words spoken in a house of mourning.

> Blessed are you . . . who are kind and deals kindly, true God and Judge, who judges with righteousness and in judgment takes [the souls of men to yourself]. . . . We are your people and your servants, and in all circumstances it is our duty to give thanks to you and to bless you. O you who repairs the breaches in Israel, may you also repair this breach in Israel, granting us life. (*Ber.* 46b)

It is, after all, the mourners who proclaim that most sublime expression of faith, the *Kaddish*. This includes the words "Blessed, praised and glorified, exalted and extolled; lauded, honored, and acclaimed be the name of the Holy One, who is ever to be praised, though far above the eulogies and songs of praise and consolation that human lips can utter; and let us say: Amen" (*Siddur Lev Chadash* 524). In acknowledging "the righteousness of God's judgment," we express faith in the outcome. "Let his great Name be blessed forever and to all eternity." That is our response to the recitation of the *Kaddish* in the house of mourning.

Modern Doubts

Doctrine is one thing; interpretation is another. The Enlightenment and the Age of Reason have left their mark on Judaism as well as on Christianity. The question often asked now is, what do the words "affirming the Resurrection" really mean? Friedlander voiced the problem: "As imperfect as is our conception of a creation from nothing, so imperfect is our notion of the Resurrection of the dead" (164). Admittedly, nature demonstrates that God gives life to the dead. But for traditional Judaism, how this will work out is a mystery. Is a pious optimism the best there is?

The Resurrection of Yeshua

Yeshua taught about Resurrection. God is the God of the living and also the God of *Avraham* (Abraham), *Yitz'chak* (Isaac), and *Ya'acov* (Jacob). It follows that the patriarchs must themselves be alive (Mark 12:26).

Yeshua also demonstrated the power to raise the dead. Others, however, had done that—for example, the prophets Elijah and Elisha. Yeshua promised eternal life to those who believed, but this was not a foreign notion to a people who believed in an afterlife. Resurrection was, after all, an issue between the Pharisees and the Sadducees.

What set the early *talmidim* on fire for God was the bodily Resurrection of Yeshua himself, never to die again. This is what the *Ruach haKodesh* energized them to preach: "God has raised him up and freed him from the suffering of death; it was impossible that death could keep its hold on him" (Acts 2:24). "God raised up this Yeshua," proclaimed Kefa (Peter). "And we are all witnesses of it!" (Acts 2:32). This Resurrection was everlasting! Here, then, was a real guarantee of eternal life.

For Thought

Yeshua rose from the dead during the Passover week, at the time of the waving of the firstfruits. *Sha'ul* spoke of the risen Yeshua as "firstfruits" (1 Cor. 15:20). He was the token, the assurance of the harvest of Resurrection life to come. We can know that we will live because Yeshua rose and lives. The Resurrection of Yeshua has proved the validity of his messiahship and of his claims to be the giver of eternal life. As Job said, "I know that my Redeemer lives. . . . I will see him for myself" (19:25, 27). This is the certainty that we have, that we may enjoy, that we must share.

The Resurrection is the hope that has fortified believers in Yeshua through the centuries. We can endure now because the light beyond the darkness is not just a desperate hope or a yearning. It is a certainty based on a historical fact—the Resurrection of Yeshua the Messiah.

> *ADONAI* is my shepherd; I lack nothing.
> He has me lie down in grassy pastures,
> he leads me by quiet water,
> he restores my inner person.
>
> He guides me in right paths
> for the sake of his own name.
> Even if I pass through death-dark ravines,

I will fear no disaster; for you are with me;
your rod and staff reassure me.

You prepare a table for me,
even as my enemies watch;
you anoint my head with oil
from an overflowing cup.

Goodness and grace will pursue me
every day of my life;
and I will live in the house of ADONAI
for years and years to come. (Ps. 23)

A Prayer

Thank you, living Lord, that your Son did not just die but he rose to life and he lives. Thank you for the assurance this gives me for myself and for my loved ones who have died in you. Thank you for the strength this certainty gives me to endure whatever comes today.

I know that my Redeemer lives, that we will see him, that we will be with him.

Blessed are you, O Lord, who makes the dead live.

Chapter 14

Blessed Be His Name

—

ברוך שמו

Barukh Shemo

—

Thou art holy, and Thy name is holy,
And those who are holy shall praise Thee every day.
Blessed art Thou, Lord, the holy God. (*Amidah* 3)

The preeminent characteristic of God is holiness. J. H. Hertz comments, "In the sublime strains of the third benediction, God is hailed as the Holy God of a Holy People, and his holiness is proclaimed on earth as it is in heaven" (*The Authorised Daily Prayer Book with Commentary* 136). Because God is holy, his name is holy. For the Jewish people, a name is not merely a label but an indication of the bearer's character. In the case of God, his name is so identified with his person that one speaks of him as *HaShem* (The Name). That is why the name of God is worthy of special reverence.

The Many Names of God

God has revealed himself to his people in many ways. His names, therefore, are numerous. He is *Elohim* (God supreme), *El Shaddai* (the Almighty), *Adonai Tzva'ot* (the Lord of hosts), and *haMakom* (the Place). He is *haKadosh* (the Holy One), *Av haRahamim* (Father of mercies), and *Av she baShamayim* (Father in heaven). He is *Havayah*—the ineffable, unspeakable Name by which he revealed himself to Moses—the timeless One, who was and is and will be forever.

There are other names. In *The Rabbinic Anthology*, we read these words:

God said to Moses, "Thou desirest to know my Name. I am called according to my deeds. When I judge my creatures, I am

called Elohim; when I wage war against the wicked, I am called
Sabaoth; when I suspend judgment for a man's sins, I am called
El Shaddai (God Almighty); but when I have compassion upon
my world, I am called Yahweh, for Yahweh means the attribute
of mercy, as it is said, 'Yahweh, Yahweh (the Lord, the Lord),
merciful and gracious' (Exod. 34:6)." . . . This is the meaning of
the words, "I AM that I AM," namely, "I am called according to
my deeds." (6)

Kiddush HaShem

Kiddush haShem (sanctification of the Name) is of great importance in
Judaism. We sanctify God's name as a congregation when we rise to recite the *Amidah,* especially in the third *b'rakhah.* We do so, as well, as
we strive to live holy lives. That is Israel's calling—to sanctify God's
Name in word and deed among the nations. "The more we fear and
love God, the deeper and more intense is our feeling of reverence for
everything which is connected in our thoughts with the Name of the
Almighty . . . this feeling of reverence . . . finds expression in our conduct" (Friedlander 276).

Israel's special obligation is to sanctify the Name in the eyes of the
nations. This is a serious responsibility. God's people fulfill it when
they conduct themselves in uprightness, justice, and lovingkindness,
making God and his ways attractive to others.

Chillul HaShem

When godly attributes are lacking, people commit *Chillul haShem*
(profanation of God's name). Saying God's name needlessly falls into
this category. According to Rabbi Johanan ben Barokah, profanation of
the name is "a sin which includes not merely impious speech but any
act or word which offends against the majesty of God" (*Av.* 4:5). *The
Rabbinic Anthology* cites this comment on Leviticus 19:15: "A judge
who perverts justice . . . defiles the land, profanes the name of God,
causes the Shechinah to depart, Israel to fall by the sword, and to be ex-
iled from their land" (384). So serious is *Chillul haShem* that the Talmud holds it to be a greater sin than idolatry (*San.* 106a).

Eric Lipson wrote that "*Kiddush haShem* displays, both to Jew and
Gentile, commitment to God, and his word. *Chillul haShem* breaks
down the relationship between Jew and Jew, between God and his *Am
Segullah* (Special Treasure)" (unpublished).

Shem L'Vatala (Saying the Name in Vain)

So holy is the Tetragrammaton (יהוה), that to speak it with phonetical correctness is considered by many to be equivalent to taking God's name in vain. Indeed, the Talmud states that such a person loses his share in the world to come (*San.* 90a). Rather than risk *Chillul haShem*, many would prefer to say "*Adonai*" or simply to use the term "*HaShem*." Although it is possible that the Jewish sages transmitted the original pronunciation to their disciples, the practice of saying the name eventually ceased, so today no one knows the true pronunciation with certainty. There is some doubt about when this prohibition began. There was a time when even the common people were encouraged to use the name openly and freely. The Mishnah records these words: "It was ordained that a man should greet his friends by mentioning the Name" (*Ber.* 9:5). There have been stories of certain *Baale Shem* (Masters of the Name) who knew the pronunciation and used it to perform miracles, but orthodoxy does not recognize these tales as truth.

Hirsch taught that, if any of the names of God have unnecessarily and inappropriately passed one's lips, one should add a phrase expressing respect, such as "Blessed be his glorious Name forever" (452). The making of a *b'rakhah* inappropriately is considered to be *Shem l'vatala*. An example of this impropriety would be making the *motzi* (blessing over bread) and then not eating bread. One should immediately say, "*Shem k'vod malkhuto l'olam va-ed*" ("Blessed is his glorious name, whose kingdom is forever and ever").

Blessing the Name

Barukh Shem and *Barukh atah haShem* are expressions of praise and thanksgiving to the Almighty. In blessing the Name, we are blessing God, the bearer of the Name. The second part of the *Sh'ma*, following the words:

שמע ישראל יהוה אלהינו יהוה אחר

Sh'ma Yisrael, Adonai Eloheynu Adonai Echad (Hear, O Israel, the Lord thy God, the Lord is One) is:

ברוך שם כבוד מלכותו לעולם ועד

Barukh Shem k'vod malkhuto l'olam va'ed (Blessed be his Name, whose glorious kingdom is forever and ever.

Sometimes, when we hear the *Shem* recited in a *b'rakhah*, we respond under our breath, "*Barukh Hu u'varukh Sh'mo*" ("Blessed be He, and blessed be his Name"). We wish, not to interrupt the proceedings, but to share in and identify with the speaker's reverence for God. It is common, when speaking God's Name, to add the words "Blessed be his Name." Maimonides does this in his *Principles*. As the congregation is called to prayer with the words "*Barukh et Adonai*" ("Bless the Lord"), we respond, "Let the Lord's Name be blessed." Likewise, as the scroll is returned to the ark after the reading of *Torah*, the reader says, "Let them praise the Name of the Lord, for his Name alone is exalted."

Messiah's Name

In the Talmud, we read that Messiah's Name existed before the sun and the stars (*Pes.* 54a). That is another way of proclaiming the preexistence of Messiah. The *B'rit Hadashah* (New Testament) puts it like this: "In the beginning was the Word, and the Word was with God, and the Word was God. He was with God in the beginning" (John 1:1–2). The most frequently used name for Messiah in the *Tanakh* is "Son of David." The blind Bar-Timai called Yeshua by this name when he cried: "Son of David! Have pity on me!" (Mark 10:47). No wonder they tried to silence him. The words were of revolutionary significance. The title also connotes the setting up a righteous kingdom.

"Redeemer" is another messianic title (Isa. 59:20). It reveals the promise of deliverance, setting free—indeed, the payment of a price. The first *b'rakhah* in the *Amidah* includes the words "God . . . will bring a redeemer to their children's children for his Name's sake." "We had hoped that he would be the one to liberate Isra'el!" wailed the two on the Emmaus road (Luke 24:21). The risen Yeshua replied, "Didn't the Messiah have to die like this before entering his glory?" (v. 26). He claimed to come on a mission of seeking and saving (19:10), of deliverance (4:21). These were redemptive tasks!

According to Klausner, Messiah's name is also "Peace" (462), referring to the passage in Isaiah that speaks of the coming of a Prince of Peace (Isa. 9:5[6]). Ginsburgh points to the words "They shall place my Name on the people of Israel"; these words follow "May ADONAI lift up his face toward you and give you peace" (Num. 6:26–27). He suggests the words mean that "Peace" is itself a name of God (143). Perhaps *Sha'ul* was thinking of this when he claimed that "he himself is our *shalom* [peace]" (Eph. 2:14). His claim was that Yeshua not only *gives* but *is shalom*.

For Thought

The name Yeshua—*Adonai* saves—comes from two Hebrew words: "salvation" and "God." Yosef (Joseph) was told to give the child this name because "he will save his people from their sins" (Matt. 1:21). Salvation was his preeminent calling; he came to seek and to save the lost. "Savior" is his most precious name to us, as we respond in love to what he has done to achieve our salvation. One day every knee will bow in honor of that name and every tongue will acknowledge him to be *ADONAI* (Phil. 2:10–11). Ultimately, all will recognize him as "KING OF KINGS AND LORD OF LORDS" (Rev. 19:16). Until then, he commands his disciples to immerse new believers into the name of the Father, the Son, and the *Ruach haKodesh*. We bear his name as a sign that we belong to him.

My soul and my flesh wait for Him and pant after Him,
My Joy and my Portion, my Cup and my Maker,
Whom when I remember and mention, I feel
That nothing is more fitted for my soul's happiness
Than blessing the Name of the Eternal God. (Gabirol, *Prayer*)

A Prayer

"The breath of every living being blesses thy Name, O Lord our God. The spirit of all flesh continuously glorifies and exalts thy remembrance, O our King. From everlasting through eternity thou art God. Besides thee we have neither king, redeemer nor savior, freeing and delivering, upholding and showing tender mercy at all times of trouble and distress. Indeed we have no king but thee" (Birkat Hashir).

Blessed are you, O Lord our God, King of the universe, who sent your Son, Yeshua—Savior, Redeemer, Adonai.

Chapter 15

The Gracious One, Who Abundantly Forgives

—

הנון המרבה לסלוח
Chanun HaMarbeh liSloach

—

Maimonides' Eleventh Principle speaks of obedience, sin, and punishment: "He, the exalted One, rewards him who obeys the commands of *Torah*, and punishes him who transgresses its prohibitions."

Our God is holy and he demands holiness of his people. However, we fall far short of the standard and therefore merit judgment. But our God is also merciful and loves to forgive. Is there a conflict in the mind of God? Our hope is that God's attribute of mercy will overcome his attribute of justice, so that forgiveness will prevail. In the sixth blessing of the *Amidah* we pray:

> Forgive us, our Father, for we have sinned,
> Pardon us, our King, for we have transgressed,
> For Thou art a pardoner and forgiver.
> Blessed art Thou, Lord, Gracious One who forgives abundantly.

The Forgiving God

The path to *selikhah* (forgiveness) is *teshuvah* (turning, or repentance). "Cause us to return, O our Father, unto thy *Torah* . . . bring us back in perfect repentance unto thy presence. Blessed art thou, O Lord, who delightest in repentance" (*Amidah* 5). Repentance is always appropriate. This is particularly the case at the time of the fall festivals. According to Jewish tradition, God weighs our good deeds against the bad on Rosh HaShanah, but his final decision is in abeyance until Yom Kippur (the

Day of Atonement). Those whose destinies are in doubt have ten days in which to achieve true repentance and so be inscribed in the book of life. Hirsch tells us that the fruit of Yom Kippur should be "confession, repentance, forgiveness, and atonement of sins" (391).

In ancient times, forgiveness was linked to blood sacrifice. The early chapters of Leviticus describe the ordinances for such sacrifices. However, since the destruction of the Temple, it has been impossible to practice the sacrificial ritual. Therefore, the rabbis have ordained that "three things avert evil decrees: prayer, charity, and repentance" (Cohen 115).

The most beautiful expression of repentance, confession, and forgiveness is Psalm 51. David was facing the gravity of his sin with Bathsheba. His actions would have repercussions in many lives and for many years to come. But primarily, he had sinned against God. He was asking for forgiveness, and that was no light thing. It would mean the complete blotting out of his sin. Though the consequences of his sin could not be undone, David asked for a new beginning in his relationship with God:

> In your great compassion, blot out my crimes. Wash me completely from my guilt, and cleanse me from my sin. . . . Create in me a clean heart, God; renew in me a resolute spirit. . . . Restore my joy in your salvation. (Ps. 51:3–4[1–2], 12[10], 14[12])

Many *selikhot* (penitential prayers) are used primarily on solemn days. On the eve of Yom Kippur, the *Kol Nidre* liturgy contains a comprehensive litany of prayers of confession. A series of equally comprehensive pleas for forgiveness follows. God's repeated response is "*Salakhti*" ("I have forgiven").

Here is a poem that is sometimes recited on Yom Kippur. Traditionally, it is ascribed to Yomtov of York in 1190, the year of the massacre of the Jews of York, England. That was a significant place and date for Jewish people to be considering the subject of forgiveness!

> Raise to thee this my plea, take my prayer,
> Sin unmake for thy sake and declare,
> "Forgiven!"
>
> Tears, regret, witness set in sin's place;
> Uplift trust from the dust to thy face—
> "Forgiven!"

Voice that sighs, tear-filled eyes, do not spurn;
Weigh and pause, plead my cause, and return
"Forgiven!"

Yea, off-rolled—as foretold—clouds impure,
Zion's folk, free of yolk, O assure
"Forgiven!"

The Duty of Forgiveness

God's nature is to have mercy and to forgive. Therefore, we, too, must practice forgiveness. *Torah* instructs us clearly, "Don't take vengeance on or bear a grudge against any of your people" (Lev. 19:18). Rabbinic teaching is also unequivocal. "Your forgiveness must be real and complete, so that no trace of rancour remains in you" (Hirsch 56). Forgetting must accompany forgiving. "Your God requires you to forget, therefore forget" (Hirsch 56).

Sometimes it is hard to forgive. In such cases, we need to go to the offending person and discuss the matter face to face in a reasonable way (Hirsch 439). It takes two sides to restore a relationship. The offending party must be ready to admit the wrong and to ask for forgiveness. The offended party must be ready to accept the apology and not nurse a grievance (Cohen 243). In the matter of forgiveness, said the sages, "a man should always be soft as a reed and not hard like a cedar" (*Taan.* 20b). Our prayer is "Teach us . . . to be generous both to forgive and to accept forgiveness" (*Siddur Lev Chadash* 202). Similarly, Colossians 3:13 states, "Bear with one another; if anyone has a complaint against someone else, forgive him. Indeed, just as the Lord has forgiven you, so you must forgive."

One problem is particularly relevant to the Jewish people. Telushkin faces it by stating that no one can forgive crimes committed against someone else (351–52). Recalling Leviticus 6, he says that even God will not forgive sins committed against another person unless the guilty one has made restitution. This is the standard answer given to those who say, "Isn't time that the Jewish people forgave for the Holocaust?" Jonathan Sacks countered this thinking during a televised Rosh HaShanah message: "Only if we have the courage to forgive will we have the strength to break free of the prison of the past." My not forgiving you ultimately hurts me more than it hurts you.

Yeshua spoke much of forgiveness. "Forgive your brother from your [heart]," he said (Matt. 18:35). Forgiveness is no shallow, easy exercise. I must practice it repeatedly and wholeheartedly. I must forgive not only my brother but my enemy too. Our example is Yeshua, who cried, "Father, forgive them; they don't understand what they are doing" (Luke 23:34).

Forgive and Be Forgiven

The rabbis teach us that there is a link between forgiveness given and forgiveness received. "He who foregoes retaliation, his sins are remitted; when his pardon is asked, he grants it" (*Yoma* 23a). "Whose sin does God forgive? He who forgives sins" (*Rosh HaShanah* 17a). Yeshua showed that he was clearly within this tradition when he said, "Forgive, and you will be forgiven" (Luke 6:37). The reverse is also true. "The man who declines to forgive, preserves the enmity and is glad when misfortune befalls the other person, becomes thereby the guilty party and God's anger is turned away from the other and directed towards himself" (Cohen 244). Likewise, says Yeshua, "If you do not forgive others their offenses, your heavenly Father will not forgive yours" (Matt. 6:15).

Hirsch goes even further, stating that we should not wait for the apology! "Be easily appeased as soon as your brother asks for forgiveness . . . he who soon forgives is soon forgiven. If you are really good . . . you will forget hurts and insults without pardon being asked of you" (56).

Yeshua and Forgiveness

Yeshua's teaching about giving and receiving forgiveness was not new. Where he broke fresh ground was in claiming the authority to forgive sins. Wasn't this God's prerogative alone? That was what upset people. Who was this man who presumed to forgive sins (Luke 7:49)?

Yeshua linked forgiveness with love. "The woman loves me much because she has been forgiven much," he said to *Shim'on* (Simon) the Pharisee. "I tell you that her sins—which are many!—have been forgiven, because she loved much" (see Luke 7:39–47). When we love, we will forgive. When we have received forgiveness, we will love.

That is why we love our Messiah Yeshua. He has procured our forgiveness. He has fulfilled the meaning of the Levitical blood sacrifices. Hence, "in union with him, through the shedding of his blood, we are set free—our sins are forgiven" (Eph. 1:7). God has forgiven because of what Messiah did. Therefore, we must forgive one another. We have no right to withhold forgiveness (4:32).

For Thought

Forgiveness is perhaps the most precious gift that God gives to me in the Messiah. It was an expensive gift. Will I reject it because I cannot bring myself to forgive a wrong done to me? I may have been harboring a grievance against someone for years; how, then, can I claim forgiveness for myself?

> Forgive your neighbor the wrong he has done,
> and then your sins will be pardoned when you pray.
> Does anyone harbor anger against another,
> and expect healing from the Lord?
> If one has no mercy toward another like himself,
> can he then seek pardon for his own sins? (Eccles. 28:2–4 NRSV)

All sin is ultimately against God, and so we have to deal with him about it. David expressed it perfectly: "Against you, you only, have I sinned and done what is evil from your perspective" (Ps. 51:6[4]).

A Prayer

Father, I want to forgive that person who hurt me. Please give me your gracious spirit of forgiveness so that I may do so. And Lord, forgive me my sins, for I forgive everyone who has wronged me.

Blessed are you, O Lord, who is gracious and abundantly forgives.

Chapter 16

The True Judge

—

דִּין הָאֱמֶת

Dayan HaEmet

—

Look upon us in our suffering,
And fight our struggles,
Redeem us speedily, for thy Name's sake,
For Thou art a mighty Redeemer.
Blessed art Thou, Lord, Redeemer of Israel. (*Amidah 7*)

The seventh *b'rakhah* in the *Amidah* recognizes the reality of suffering. We all experience seasons of darkness and bewilderment. We all struggle with burdens from time to time and have to fend off despair. These experiences are a part of life. The *Siddur Lev Chadash* puts it like this: "If the duration of sorrows and the patience with which they are borne ennoble, the Jews can challenge the aristocracy of every land" (265).

Blessings in Suffering

The rabbis have always taught that one may accept suffering as a mark of God's special love (Cohen 64). In *The Mystery of Pain*, S. Alfred Adler (1875–1910) noted, "They call God's chastisements the blessed scourgings of love" (Hertz, *Jewish Thoughts* 296). Therefore, it is appropriate to thank God for our sufferings. They are God's precious gift, sent to be the means of our development. Hirsch taught that one should examine oneself to see if the suffering was a deserved punishment. If one could find no sin, he offered another explanation. "Know that your sufferings are chastisements of love that God sends upon you because He loves you and because you love Him, in order to reinforce your love of God, to exalt you by trial, to perfect you and, when you are perfected, to set you up as a pattern" (39). Even the Messiah needed to be made "perfect [that is, able to accomplish his goal] through suffering" (Heb. 2:10 NIV). Likewise, we understand that "even gold is tested for genuineness by fire. The purpose of these trials is so that your trust's genuineness . . . will be judged worthy of praise, glory and honor at the revealing of Yeshua the Messiah" (1 Pet. 1:7).

"Don't speak impulsively—don't be in a hurry to give voice to your words before God. For God is in heaven, and you are on earth; so let your words be few" (Eccles. 5:1[2]). Better by far to learn to make a *b'rakhah* for the bad as for the good: "*ADONAI* gave, *ADONAI* took; blessed be the name of *ADONAI*" (Job 1:21). For good experiences one may say, "Blessed are you . . . who are good and dispenses good," while for bad ones the words are "Blessed be the true judge" (*Ber.* 9:5). The thought behind this is that when we make a *b'rakhah* we are not only saying "thank you"; we are also expressing the strength of our relationship with the Almighty (Forst 24).

It is not easy to attain such heights of spirituality in practice. Often we settle for the second best of resignation. If we can endure suffering with silent resignation, at least we will avoid bitterness. "When to bear our griefs becomes our part, let faith and hope exhort us—God knows best" (Green, "Resignation").

The Purpose of Suffering

If one views suffering as purposeful rather than random, it is easier to endure. The Hebrew word for suffering (*jisur*) comes from the same root as that for instruction (*musar*). The Baal Shem Tov taught that suffering makes us more sensitive and compassionate (Newman 485). Other rabbis have put it differently. The Kobriner said that one should take it as a bitter medicine prescribed by the doctor to promote healing (Newman 483). The Bratzlaver's explanation for suffering was this: "Man is born, not to enjoy the world and its pleasures, but to labor for his eternal life. Tribulation is one of the tools intended for this purpose" (Newman 126).

Sacks tackles the problem that this outlook raises for Judaism today. He reminds us that we can look back to the Egypt experience and know that it pointed to the Promised Land and nationhood. However, he says, "so far, it is not apparent to all Jewry just what the Holocaust points to. This is part of the continuing pain and bewilderment" (Sacks 154).

Chastening can also be a positive experience, as several analogies make clear. Salt is one example. As salt sweetens meat, says the Talmud, so chastenings can purge iniquities (*Ber.* 5a). Heat offers another analogy. "As oil is made good only by heating, so only through sufferings does Israel repent" (Montefiore and Loewe 165). Still another analogy is pressure. "As the olive yields its oil only by hard pressure, so the Israelites do not return to righteousness except through suffering" (Montefiore and Loewe 95). Hirsch suggests that suffering may even be a privilege, a mark of approval: "To those who are capable of improvement God gives suffering in order that they may improve themselves" (31). The *Tanakh* supports this view of suffering. Scripture gives us the image of the refiner of silver. "You, God, have tested us, refined us as silver is refined" (Ps. 66:10). The rabbis call such sufferings "chastenings of love" (*Ber.* 5a).

Suffering as Atonement

Some forms of suffering—notably plagues and childlessness—have been regarded by some as "an altar of atonement" (*Ber.* 5b). They may secure forgiveness even as the sacrifices did in Temple times (Cohen 113). However, in Jewish thought, there is strong resistance to the idea of vicarious suffering, though Cohen acknowledges that sometimes it seems the good do suffer for the sins of the wicked (Cohen 125).

Louis Jacobs explains that God has so ordered things that our deeds influence and affect others. "Is not this very fact a constant reminder that God wants man to belong to his fellows and possess a sense of responsibility to them?" (Jacobs, *Principles* 366). He cites two Bible passages. The first is Abraham's cry: "Will you actually sweep away the righteous with the wicked?" (Gen. 18:23). The second Bible passage is Aaron's protest: "Oh God, . . . if one person sins, are you going to be angry with the entire assembly?" (Num. 16:22).

Enduring, Not Enjoying, Suffering

Even those who are righteous experience pain. God does not expect us to *enjoy* suffering (*Ber.* 5b). He allows us—even expects us—to weep. This is the reason why the days after the death of a loved one are set aside for grieving. We should not attempt to offer easy comfort while a loss is fresh and raw.

Suffering as Punishment

Some rabbis have suggested that suffering may be a punishment for the neglect of *Torah*. "Everyone who is able to occupy himself with *Torah* and does not do so, the Holy One, blessed be He, brings upon him dreadful sufferings to stir him" (Simeon ben Lakish, *Ber.* 5a). The belief that there is no suffering without iniquity is based on the conviction of the fundamental justice of God. Maimonides was a proponent of this view. His Eleventh Principle states, "He, the exalted One, rewards him who obeys the commands of the *Torah*, and punishes him who transgresses its prohibitions."

Those who hold this view are aware of the difficulty with it: why do the righteous suffer and the wicked prosper? The problem becomes less acute if one sees reward and punishment as being carried out in the next world as well as in this one. Then "there is reward and punishment both in this world, and in the next . . . reward and punishment are both corporeal and spiritual" (Jacobs, *Principles* 361). The rabbinic writings cover a broad spectrum of viewpoints in discussing this subject. Jacobs's comment is this: "To attempt even to cover the whole range of rabbinic views on the subject of reward and punishment is virtually an impossible task" (*Principles* 355).

The Problem of Suffering

Question: "My God, my God, why are my sighs hidden from you?"

Answer: "It is not in our power to explain either the prosperity of the wicked or the afflictions of the righteous" (*Av.* 4:19).

We do not know why these things happen.

As for the Holocaust, it is "a mystery wrapped in silence" (Sacks 139). "We are not yet ready to say where it belongs in the drama between God and his people" (Sacks 141). Sometimes God is active in affliction. Sometimes he is passive, allowing person to afflict person, and so the innocent suffer (Sacks 148–49).

The Right Response to Suffering

We cannot escape suffering, but we can seek to find strength to live with it and to find God in it. "People are born for trouble as surely as sparks fly upward" (Job 5:7). "Every man on earth must encounter tribulations and pain. If he takes refuge from them in the Lord, he will be comforted" (Newman 126).

> All who are sick at heart and cry in bitterness,
> Let not your soul complain in grief.
> Enter the garden of my songs, and find balm
> For your sorrow, and there sing with open mouth.
> (*Siddur Lev Chadash* 267)

God Suffers with Us

"The divine countenance is etched with the suffering of all humanity, and we feel the comfort of knowing we are not alone" (*Siddur Lev*

Chadash 267). God is seen as suffering with his people Israel—weeping over their tribulations (Sacks 148). "God still lives," said Hirsch. "He is your God, and as the twinkling of the stars shines through the roof of foliage [the *sukkah*] so does He with His watchful eye embrace you in lovingkindness, behold your suffering, behold your tears, hear your sighs and know your cares" (125).

In times of suffering, we need to hold fast, trusting that God has not abandoned us and will not fail us. Sometimes this is very difficult. Sacks, in his wrestling with the problem of the Holocaust, admits that we may never understand, but he counsels us to remember the words of Isaiah 55:8: " 'My thoughts are not your thoughts, and your ways are not my ways,' says ADONAI" (146–47).

Helping One Another Through Times of Suffering

The sense of *mishpochah* (family, or community) is strong among Jewish people. In healthy communities, we take comfort and strength from one another during difficult times. Sometimes, our pain is such that faith struggles to survive and, if we were alone in it, we would fall:

> The night is dark
> And I am blind.
> The wind tears the stick
> from my hand. (Leivick, *The Night is Dark*)

When someone else comes alongside to walk with us and share the load of pain, it becomes more bearable:

> I hear the touch
> of someone's hand:
> Allow me to carry
> your heavy load. (Leivick, *The Night is Dark*)

Yeshua: Anointed to Heal, Liberate, and Comfort

Isaiah had assured Israel of God's continuing concern and their eventual deliverance (Isa. 61:1–3). At the beginning of his ministry, Yeshua identified himself with these words of comfort and promise (Luke 4:18–21). He was reinforcing the prophet's message and stating that the promise was now turning into actuality. As the next three years unfolded, his claims must have seemed somewhat thin, but his Resurrection validated them convincingly. He who triumphs over death can indeed assure us that suffering does not have the last word.

Yeshua was no stranger to suffering. In his life, he experienced mis-
understanding, loneliness, disappointments, and persecution. In his
dying, he endured unspeakable torment. Yet he could say, "How blessed
are those who mourn! . . . How blessed are those who are persecuted!
. . . How blessed you are when people insult you and persecute you
and tell all kinds of vicious lies about you because you follow me!"
(Matt. 5:4, 10–11). How can suffering be a blessing? Surely it is just
something we have to accept and endure as best as we can. No! "Rejoice," says Yeshua, "be glad, because your reward in heaven is great"
(Matt. 5:12). As we share in his sufferings now, we can be sure that we
will share in his glory in the time to come. That is a certainty, not a
vague hope.

For Thought

The rabbis taught extensively about the reasons for suffering and
about the right way to respond. Yeshua, our crucified Messiah, gives us
more. He is a companion in our pain. He has been there; he under-
stands, he feels, and he identifies with us. Yeshua, our risen Messiah,
offers us the possibility of turning disaster into victory, of being trans-
formed by our sufferings. Yeshua, our glorified Messiah, holds out to us
the certainty that one day all of our experiences will make sense. I can
do more than passively endure; I can triumph.

God is indeed the true Judge. I can trust him with my life now. I
can trust him with my eternal well-being.

Be still before ADONAI;
wait patiently till he comes.
Don't be upset by those whose way
succeeds because of their wicked plans.
Stop being angry, put aside rage,
and don't be upset—it leads to evil. (Ps. 37:7–8)

A Prayer

*Lord, it is in the darkness that I most appreciate your light. It is in the
emptiness that I most appreciate your presence. It is in the devastation
that I most appreciate your order and your ways. It is in my failure that I
most appreciate your victory, my Lord and my God.*

Blessed are you, O Lord, the true Judge.

Chapter 17

Who Causes the Horn of Salvation to Flourish

—

מַצְמִיחַ קֶרֶן יְשׁוּעָה
Matz'micha Keren Yeshuah

—

Speedily cause the offspring of David, thy servant, to flourish, and let his horn be exalted by thy salvation, because we wait for thy salvation all the day. Blessed art thou, O Lord, who causest the horn of salvation to flourish. (*Amidah* 15)

Messiah's Coming

The fifteenth *b'rakhah* of the *Amidah* concerns the coming of the Messiah. He is anointed to bring salvation. This longed-for salvation is associated with the liberation of the Jewish people from oppression. It will accompany a return to *HaEretz* (The Land), the restoration of the Davidic dynasty, and the rebuilding of the Temple. However, the mission of Messiah will be more far-reaching. He will come "to redeem Israel from its servitude and from all its tribulations and to bring salvation to all humanity through the salvation of Israel" (Klausner 12). No one can know when Messiah will come. It is not permissible either to calculate or to manipulate Scripture to deduce the date of his coming (Jacobs, *Principles* 368).

The Messiah is a crucial figure within Judaism, and his coming to the world is an all-important hope. As Maimonides' Twelfth Principle states, "I believe with perfect faith in the coming of the Messiah and, though he tarry, I will wait daily for his coming."

The Person and Personality of Messiah

The Talmud states that Messiah is one of seven things created before the world came into being (*Pes.* 54a). Nevertheless, he is most definitely human, not God. Klausner denies emphatically that Messiah is divine. His character, he says, "goes beyond the realm of human nature" (465). Therefore, "his kingdom is definitely a kingdom *of this world*" (466). Jacobs goes further. He states that the Messiah will not be a redeemer, because only God can redeem. The Messiah-king will be "only the leader of the redeemed people who will execute justice and righteousness upon earth" (*Principles* 373).

The personality of the Messiah will be exemplary. He will achieve the highest heights of humanity in character and in deeds. *Sanhedrin* 93b states that Isaiah is speaking of Messiah in the following verses: "The spirit of the Lord shall rest upon him, the spirit of wisdom and understanding, the spirit of counsel and might, the spirit of knowledge and of the fear of the Lord" (see Isa. 11:2). Klausner's comment on this passage is that he "will inherit the six gifts of the Holy Spirit" (467). This is how we will recognize him when he comes.

A Suffering Messiah?

Christians find it difficult to understand why Jewish people do not recognize the messiahship of Yeshua from the words of the fifty-third chapter of Isaiah. Though traditional Judaism has not been comfortable with the idea of a suffering Messiah, it has recognized such a concept in the past. It is present in the "two Messiahs" idea. Messiah ben Joseph will suffer and die, whereas Messiah ben David will triumph and reign (Klausner 496–97). Most rabbis do not see Isaiah's suffering servant in messianic terms. Rather, they identify him as the nation of Israel.

The Messianic Age

The Messiah will usher in an era of righteousness and peace. This expectation is so strong that over the course of the centuries many have fixed their hopes on the messianic age rather than on the Messiah himself. What we should look for, people have argued, is a regime of political freedom, moral superiority, social justice, and above all—peace. This peace will be for the whole human race, not only Israel. However, the Talmud clearly associates the messianic age with a person and sees his eventual coming as beyond doubt (*Ber.* 1:5).

The scenario one can deduce from the *Tanakh* begins with a time of judgment and suffering in punishment for sin (the "birth pangs" of the Messiah). Then follows a time of national repentance. After this, the Messiah will come and gather a remnant of the exiles. Messiah will abolish war, establishing a reign of righteousness, justice, and mercy. Some have associated this time with the giving of sight to the blind and hearing to the deaf, with the lame leaping and the mute singing (Isa. 35:5–6). In other circles, there has been strong resistance to the idea of a miracle-working Messiah. By the time of Yeshua, the expectation was that Elijah would come first. Perhaps he would even be the one to anoint the Messiah. Hence, the custom developed of leaving an empty chair and a full cup for Elijah at the Passover *seder*.

The Messianic Idea

The messianic hope includes political as well as spiritual longings. Hence, says Klausner, the idea of two Messiahs developed. *Mashiach ben Joseph* will be the political leader, and *Mashiach ben David* the spiritual deliverer (11). However, there have been other voices. Hillel declared, "There shall be no Messiah for Israel, because they have already enjoyed him in the days of Hezekiah" (*San.* 99a). Others have strongly disputed that view. In recent times, Jonathan Sacks has said that the messianic idea is central to Judaism. It "dictates a life lived toward the future, just as the concept of revelation dictates a life lived toward the past. Judaism is defined between the twin poles of memory and anticipation" (91).

Yeshua, *the* Messiah

"Without the Jewish Messiah, Judaism is defective; without the Christian Messiah, Christianity does not exist at all" (Klausner 530). Klausner's comment is most perceptive. To believers in Yeshua, his messianic identity is not just one idea among many; it is central. He is everything, the only means of our salvation. He is the only object of our adoration. That is why we call ourselves "Messianic."

In the *B'rit Hadashah*, we see the partial fulfillment of many of the promises of the *Tanakh* as well as the expectations of rabbinic tradition. The fulfillment is partial because there is more to come. When Messiah returns, he will complete the picture.

Shim'on knew he was holding the Messiah in his arms. "I have seen with my own eyes your *yeshu'ah* [salvation]" (Luke 2:30). Yeshua himself claimed to be the anointed one spoken of by the prophet Isaiah (Luke 4:18–21).

Some acknowledged Yeshua's messiahship by naming him "Son of David." That was the most common title for the Messiah. They believed that the miracles spoke for themselves (Matt. 9:27). Both *Shim'on Kefa* (Simon Peter) and Marta (Martha) were among this number. When brought to a point of decision, they responded with the declaration "You are the *Mashiach*, the Son of the living God" (Matt. 16:16).

Yeshua used *Kefa*'s declaration to lead straight into teaching about his coming suffering and death. He wanted them to understand that, in the short term, the path led downhill.

After his resurrection, he rebuked the two on the *Amma'us* (Emmaus) road: "Foolish people! So unwilling to put your trust in everything the prophets spoke! Didn't the Messiah have to die like this before entering his glory?" (Luke 24:25–26). He then backed up his words from different parts of the *Tanakh*.

The Ethiopian eunuch found the words of Isaiah 53 remarkable. "Is the prophet talking about himself or someone else?" he asked Philip. There was no question in his mind but that the subject of the text was an individual. Philip was quite clear in his answer. "Beginning with that passage, he went on to tell him the Good News about Yeshua" (Acts 8:32–35).

Yeshua hinted at his preexistence in the words "Before Abraham came into being, I AM!" (John 8:58). Yochanan understood this truth. "The Word was . . . with God in the beginning. . . . The Word became a human being and lived with us" (John 1:2, 14).

People marveled that no one ever spoke like this man before (John 7:46). His miracles offered evidence of his nature. When Yochanan the Immerser's followers came to Yeshua to ask if he was the expected one, he sent them back with a clear message. "Go, tell Yochanan what you have been seeing and hearing: the blind are seeing again, the lame are walking, people with *tzara'at* [leprosy] are being cleansed, the deaf are hearing, the dead are being raised, the Good News is being told to the poor" (Luke 7:22).

Traditional expectations of Messiah differed from reality. The writer to Messianic Jews (Hebrews) states that the one who was with God before creation, and who provided purification for sins, was God's own Son (Heb. 1:2–3). Yochanan wrote that the one who was with God in the beginning, and who lived among us, was no less than God Himself (John 1:1).

Yeshua taught at length about the messianic kingdom, but he saw it in less earthly terms than Judaism finds acceptable. For him, the kingdom was not primarily concerned with this world (John 18:36). The kingdom is within and among ordinary people in everyday situations (Luke 17:21). For many Jewish people, seemingly locked into a cycle of disaster and pain, that is not good enough. The promise of inner peace is meaningful when you have it but incomprehensible when you do not (John 14:27).

Yeshua's identity as Messiah makes complete sense only in the context of the future. The promises have not all been fulfilled. The world is not at peace. The visible Christian Church, to its shame, has often brought more pain than gain to the Jewish people. The New Covenant of Jeremiah has not been fully revealed. We wait for another messianic coming. "This Yeshua, who has been taken away from you into heaven, will come back to you in just the same way as you saw him go into heaven" (Acts 1:11). The messianic age that is coming will be glorious beyond all imagining (1 Cor. 2:9). On the throne will be the Messiah—Yeshua. This is the hope that messianic believers—both Jewish and non-Jewish—embrace.

The proclamations and events surrounding his birth were startling. His claims, his character, and his deeds defied explanation. His teaching, his death, and his resurrection were unique. All these speak of one who was either a charlatan or the genuine article. Others have written at length to prove that Yeshua is the Messiah. It is not the purpose of this book to add to their number. The important question is this: if we believe that the case for his messiahship has been proven, what are the implications for our lives?

For Thought

If it is true that "God has made him both Lord and Messiah—this Yeshua" (Acts 2:36), then nothing can ever be the same again. Our focus is now on a person who suffered and died to procure our forgiveness and our life. All our hopes now rest on him whose name is "salvation." He is our only security. One day he will return to establish the messianic kingdom of righteousness and peace. In the meantime, he claims total authority over us as Lord.

The question "Who am I?" absorbs many in Western society. This question is insignificant beside the larger question "Who is Yeshua?" If he is who he claimed to be, then he deserves to be the center and focus of our lives. Then the question "Who am I?" will lose its urgency. I am who I am in him. Ultimately, nothing else matters.

A child is born to us,
a son is given to us;
dominion will rest on his shoulders,
and he will be given the name
Pele-Yo'etz El Gibbor
Avi-'Ad Sar-Shalom
[Wonder of a Counselor, Mighty God,
Father of Eternity, Prince of Peace]. (Isa. 9:5[6])

A Prayer

Yeshua, my Messiah, my Savior, and my Lord, be the center of my life. Be the voice I hear in the night, the light I see in the morning. Be the hand I reach out to, the treasure I hold most dear. Be all to me and be in all for me.

Blessed are you, O Lord our God, King of the universe, who has sent Yeshua, your Son, to be our Savior, our Redeemer—our Messiah.

Chapter 18

Who Restores His Divine Presence to Zion

—

המחזיר שכינתו לציון
HaMachazir Sh'khinato l'Tzion

—

Favorably receive, O Lord our God, Thy people Israel and their
prayer,
Restore the worship to Thy Temple in Zion,
Receive with love and favor the offerings of Israel and their
prayer,
And may the worship of Thy people Israel always be favorably
received by Thee.
May our eyes behold Thy return to Zion in mercy.
Blessed art Thou, Lord, who restores His Divine Presence to
Zion. (*Amidah* 17)

A Love Affair

"Over and over again in the Talmud," states Abraham Cohen, "stress is
laid upon the intimate and unique relationship that exists between God
and His people" (62). This special relationship is one of the threads running through the entire Bible. God describes Israel as "my firstborn son"
and "the very pupil of my eye" (Exod. 4:22; Zech. 2:12[8]). In a time of
failure, God's cry to Israel was "Of all the families on earth, only you
have I intimately known" (Amos 3:2). Talmudic claims about the
uniqueness and intimacy of the relationship between God and Israel
rest upon the *Tanakh*. It is a love relationship. At its best, the love is on
both sides: "The rabbis believed that God and Israel were united by a
passionate love on both sides" (Montefiore and Loewe 58). At times,
there even seems to be a suggestion that God's continuing love is

contingent upon Israel's continuing love. "You have made me the only object of your love in the world, so I shall make you the only object of my love in the world to come" (*Ber.* 6a).

God's Love for Israel

God has demonstrated his love for Israel in many ways. His redemptive acts at the Exodus from Egypt were for a specific purpose—that he might live among his people. "They are to make me a sanctuary, so that I may live among them" (Exod. 25:8). The *Sh'khinah* was a mark of his favor, the visible representation of his presence. His people possess a confident expectation that God will restore his presence. "Blessed are you, O Lord," says the seventeenth *b'rakhah* of the *Amidah*, quoted above, "who restores your divine presence to Zion."

God showed his love to Israel in another way—he entrusted them with the *Torah* at Sinai. "Beloved are Israel, for they were called children of the All-present . . . for unto them was given the desirable instrument [*Torah*]" (*Av.* 3:18). Israel sees this mark of trust and love as a great privilege as well as a responsibility.

God will always be a faithful lover, true to his covenant and his promises. "The Lord our God and the God of our fathers for all eternity . . . the Strength of our lives, the Shield of our deliverance" (*Amidah* 18). He will always be there for us when we call upon him. "Thou art a God who hears prayers . . . Thou hearest the prayer of Thy people Israel with compassion" (*Amidah* 16). The liturgy is full of this confidence. No matter what disasters befall, the certainty of God's faithfulness to Israel looks to the ultimate future. "All Israel has a share in the world to come" (*San.* 10:1), because the love of God for Israel is an "everlasting love" (Jer. 31:2[3]), a mother love (Isa. 49:15). What love could be more permanent? What love could be stronger?

Many have asked, why did God choose this particular people? The *Tanakh* makes it clear that the choice was not based on merit. Was it favoritism? The rabbis have felt it necessary to offer some sort of explanation that does not present God as unjust. According to Jewish tradition, the *Torah* was first offered to all the other nations but they, one after another, refused the privilege. Only then did God turn to little Israel, who accepted the burden (Cohen 65).

Israel's Love for God

Israel has had a deep sense of gratitude for being God's chosen people. This gratitude is accompanied by a sense of privilege for being entrusted with *Torah*: "By the light of Thy presence have you given us . . . a Torah of life" (*Amidah* 19). The proper response to love is love: "You are to love ADONAI your God with all your heart, all your being and all your resources" (Deut. 6:5). Among the Hasidim, joy, dance, and spontaneity characterize worship and demonstrate the love of God. However, most rabbis have taught that we show love for God by our observance of *Torah* (Cohen 142). They are referring to the entire *Tanakh* as well as the talmudic tradition. In other words, what we do is of more value than what we feel or believe. Yeshua taught, "If you love me, you will keep my commands" (John 14:15). Likewise, we read, "Faith by itself, unaccompanied by actions, is dead" (James 2:17).

Israel's Longings

Israel's longings arise from the promises of the *Tanakh*. Central to these longings have been those promises concerned with the land of Israel. Telushkin puts it this way: "The land is central to the relationship between God and the Jews" (567). This yearning for the land has echoed through two thousand years of exile. Judah Halevi, the twelfth-century Spanish poet, expressed it lyrically: "My heart is in the East, and I am in the furthermost West. How then can I taste what I eat? And how can food be sweet to me . . . while Zion is in fetters . . . and I am in Arab chains?" (*My Heart is in the East*) Even for those who were able to travel to the Land, there was no comfort in seeing its desolation.

> We raised our eyes to see her but could not recognize her, so wasted did she look. She had lost her shape, her form was gone; she was bound in chains and weighed down by her fetters. We raised our voices in lament for the desecration of Mount Moriah. ("Lament for Zion," anonymous tenth-century poem)

That longing still finds expression in the familiar words spoken toward the close of the Passover *seder*: "*L' shanah haba'ah b'Yerushalayim*" ("Next year in Jerusalem").

The Temple is central to the longing for the land and the city: "Restore the worship to Thy Temple in Zion" (*Amidah* 17). With the rebuilding of the Temple will come the return of God's presence to Zion. "The name of the city will be ADONAI Shamah [ADONAI is there]" (Ezek. 48:35). The Messiah will come and establish the reign of righteousness (*Amidah* 15). Then will come the peace and justice for which Israel has so long cried. "Establish peace, well-being, blessing, grace, loving kindness, and mercy upon us, and upon all Israel Thy people" (*Amidah* 19). "Rule over us, Thou alone, O Lord with kindness and mercy, and vindicate us in the judgment" (*Amidah* 11). The Jewish people long for peace in a world where they have never been safe. They long for justice in a world where they have always been the oppressed. They long for their Land in a world where they have for so long been wanderers and seen as intruders, "like a vessel nobody wants" (Hos. 8:8).

The Meaning of Chosenness

Chosenness is not favoritism. God loves the entire human race: "That the righteous of all peoples will inherit the bliss of the Hereafter is the accepted doctrine of rabbinic Judaism" (Cohen 71). God's choice of Israel does not mean that he hates or rejects everyone else. Neither do Jewish people believe that Israel is superior in any way: "Chosenness has nothing in common with doctrines of racial or ethnic superiority" (Telushkin 298).

God made his purpose clear to Abraham: "By you all the families of the earth will be blessed" (Gen. 12:3). Isaiah reissued the charge: "I will also make you a light to the nations, so my salvation can spread to the ends of the earth" (Isa. 49:6). God chose Israel to be a beacon to the peoples of the world, to be the medium through which God's blessing would reach out to all. Sometimes the darkness of suffering has obscured the vision. However, it has never been totally forgotten. Isidore Epstein stated, "Before our ancestors took their stand at the foot of Mount Sinai to receive the Law, they were invited to become not only a holy nation but also a kingdom of priests, acting as priests for the rest of mankind" (89). Included in the priestly ministry has been guarding and sharing *Torah* as well as being a witness to the unique, holy, righteous God. These have been Israel's supreme gifts to the world. "We must indeed regard it as a great privilege to have been chosen by God to be the principal builders of his kingdom . . . but this privilege carries with it great responsibilities" (Epstein 93–94).

Chosenness Is Uncomfortable Sometimes

An old Yiddish proverb goes like this: "You have chosen us from among all nations—what, O God, did you have against us?" Tevye, in *Fiddler on the Roof*, protested to God, "Once in a while, can't you choose someone else?"

Chosenness was never intended by God to be the passport to an easy life. It has always carried enormous responsibilities and demanded the highest standards for Israel. God testified to his people, "Of all the families of earth, only you have I intimately known. That is why I will punish you for all your crimes" (Amos 3:2). The people who represent God as his priesthood must be like him; otherwise, the world sees a distorted image. God has had to work on his people: "I have refined you, . . . tested you in the furnace of affliction" (Isa. 48:10). Suffering has been the lot of Israel. Recognizing this, the rabbis have ruefully acknowledged, "Three precious gifts did the Holy One, blessed be he, bestow upon Israel, and all of them he gave only through the medium of suffering. They are *Torah*, the land of Israel, and the World to Come" (*Ber.* 5a).

Yeshua and the Jewish People

Yeshua came to the Jewish people embodying the fulfillment of all their hopes—for themselves and for the world. Some of this fulfillment has been experienced already; other aspects are yet to come. We see him weeping over Jerusalem because he is Jewish and he loves Jerusalem. We see him touching and transforming Gentiles as well as Jews because he loves all people. His Father sent him, "so that everyone who trusts in him may have eternal life" (John 3:16).

This universal mission, however, did not cancel Israel's calling. *Sha'ul* saw clearly that Israel's task was unfinished. Israel's "casting Yeshua aside" has led to the bringing of many Gentiles into the Kingdom. Just think, he argued, what Israel's receiving him will mean! Surely that will be nothing less than "life from the dead" (Rom. 11:15). This is not just a pious hope. Israel surely will receive Messiah Yeshua, the Savior, and "all Isra'el will be saved" (Rom. 11:26).

Some may wish that Israel would simply disappear. Many in the Church claim to have displaced Israel as God's chosen people. However, the *B'rit Hadashah* lends no credence to these imaginings, for "God's free gifts and his calling are irrevocable" (Rom. 11:29). Israel remains God's chosen.

For Thought

Being a Jewish believer in Yeshua can be confusing. The Jewish community says, "That's impossible. You cannot be Jewish and believe in Jesus." The Church alternates between a sentimental "How wonderful" and an insensitive "Now that you believe, you're no longer Jewish." No wonder that Messianic Jews frequently seek the company of other Messianic Jews. Being Jewish is a communal experience. However, let us not lose sight of the purpose of choice. In these days, why is God calling out this Messianic Jewish remnant? How can this minority within a minority fulfill his purposes, not only within Israel, but also among the worldwide Body of Messiah? We need to wrestle with these questions.

This is what ADONAI says,
who gives the sun as light for the day,
who ordained the laws for the moon and stars
to provide light for the night,
who stirs up the sea until its waves roar—
ADONAI-Tzva'ot is his name:
"If these laws leave my presence," says ADONAI,
"then the offspring of Isra'el will stop being
a nation in my presence forever."

This is what ADONAI says:
"If the sky above can be measured
and the foundations of the earth be fathomed,
then I will reject all the offspring of Isra'el
for all that they have done," says ADONAI. (Jer. 31:34–36[35–37])

A Prayer

Lord, help me to see, from your perspective, what is happening in the land of Israel. Show me and the community of which I am a part our role in the Body of Messiah, so that we may soon see the fulfillment of all your purposes.

May your blessing rest upon your people Israel. May the light of your presence, your Sh'khinah, hover over us. You have given us so much. You have given the world so much through us. May we be a true reflection of your holiness, your righteousness, your graciousness, and your love. Restore, O Lord, your people Israel to yourself, and grant us your peace. Blessed are you, O Lord, who will restore your divine presence to Zion.

Final Thoughts—Cultivating a Heart for God

> May the words of my mouth and the thoughts of my heart be acceptable in your presence, ADONAI, my Rock and Redeemer. (Ps. 19:15[14])

"A *b'rakhah* is not a mindless incantation" (Forst 67). Attitude is all-important. These concluding words of the *Amidah*, from the last verse of Psalm 19, reaffirm the conviction that words alone are not enough; the attitude of my heart and my inner thought life must also be pleasing to God. The *Amidah* ends with a time of silent prayer that has inspired many gems of devotional thought. We find some of them in *B'rakhot* 16b and 17a. Rabbi Eleazar said, "May it be thy will, O Lord our God . . . that the reverence of thy Name be ever the longing of our heart." Rabbi Alexander expressed this thought more poetically. "May it be thy will, O Lord our God, to place us in a corner of light and not in a corner of darkness; and may our hearts not grow faint, nor our eyes dim." This reminds us of the words of Yeshua: "I am the light of the world; whoever follows me will never walk in darkness but will have the light which gives life" (John 8:12). Listen to Rabbi Chiyya: "May thy Torah be our occupation, and make us wholehearted in reverencing thee." It is not enough to merely abstain from evil; we must be proactive and do what is good (Ps. 34:15[14]). Perhaps best known is the prayer of Mar ben Rabina, which became incorporated into the concluding meditation during the fourth century C.E.:

> My God, guard my tongue from evil, and my lips from speaking with deceit.
> Let my soul be silent to them that curse me; yea, let my soul be as the dust unto all.
> Open my heart to thy Torah, and let my soul pursue thy commandments.
> And all who think evil against me, quickly annul their designs and frustrate their intentions.

Guarding the Tongue

Silence under persecution is not easy, as Jewish people have had ample opportunity to discover. Messianic Jews have often experienced the pain of being seen as outcasts by the Jewish community. For those who experience rejection because of their faith, Yeshua has a word: "Blessed are those who are persecuted because they pursue righteousness!" (Matt. 5:10).

Lashon hara (an evil tongue) is a major cause of disruption in human relationships. Donin states, "There is nothing more crucial to the true spiritual life and the establishment of harmony among people than controlling the tongue" (105). As we have just prayed for the peace of all Israel (*Amidah* 19), we recognize our own required contribution to that peace in the community. James was in tune with Jewish thought when he wrote, "Anyone who thinks he is religiously observant but does not control his tongue is deceiving himself, and his observance counts for nothing" (James 1:26).

Later, an additional prayer was added to the concluding words of the *Amidah*:

> Do it for the sake of thy Name, for the sake of thy might, for the sake of thy holiness, for the sake of thy *Torah*. In order that thy loved ones may be saved, save me through thy might and answer my prayer. May the words of my mouth and the meditation of my heart be acceptable to thee, O God my Strength and my Redeemer. May he who makes peace in the heavens, make peace for us and for all Israel, and say Amen.

Devekut

The root of the word *devekut* means to cling, to cleave, or to keep close. Forst translates it as "attachment to God" (25). In Deuteronomy 11:22, we read that God requires his people to love the Lord, to follow all his ways, and to cling to him. Yeshua reckoned that the commandment to love God with all one's heart, soul, and strength is the greatest of all the *mitzvot* (Matt. 22:37–38).

There has been some discussion about the meaning of the instruction to cling to God. Ibn Ezra's interpretation was that *devekut* is something that will not be achieved until death. Maimonides taught that most of us can achieve *devekut* only in the private place of prayer. Nachmanides, on the other hand, said that the commandment is for now, that *devekut* means being mindful of God and his love all the time, in every area of life. Whatever we are doing, he said, we are conscious of being in the presence of God. Sacks comments, "The suffusion of man's social existence with his covenantal intimacy with God is for Nachmanides a this-worldly possibility." It was the Hasidim, however, who brought the possibility of achieving *devekut* into the lives of ordinary members of the community. They believe it is possible for every Jewish person to know right now what it is to cling to God (Sacks 240–41).

Sha'ul, like Ibn Ezra, shows an awareness that there is a dimension of spiritual experience we cannot know until after our death: "To go off and be with the Messiah—that is better by far" (Phil. 1:23). However, *Sha'ul* kept his feet firmly planted on the ground. For him, as for Nachmanides, it was important that, while one studies *Torah* and engages in public worship, *everything* one does or says should be in the Lord's name (Col. 3:17).

Devekut has been the goal of the Jewish people. The Talmud exhorts us to read and study *Torah*, not as a means to an end, but purely as an act of love. This is what it means to have God's words written on the table of one's heart (*Nedarim* 62a). It is part of the New Covenant promise, of which Yeshua claimed to be the fulfillment. Only God himself can write his *Torah* on our hearts. However, he needs our cooperation, our desire, our love—in short, our *devekut*. The poet Judah Halevi put it like this:

Ever since you were the home of love for me,
my love has lived where you have lived. (*The Home of Love*)

When I am far from you my life is death;
but if I cling to you, my death is life. (*For the Day of Atonement*)

The early Hasidim believed that *devekut* was a missing dimension in traditional Judaism. They saw a difference between studying *Torah* and living a life of attachment to, and love for, God. The one is of the mind, while the other is of the heart. The mind can be cold; the heart should burn with enthusiasm for God. For the Hasidim, *devekut* means that "ideally man should always have God in his thoughts, seeing beneath appearances only the divine vitality which infuses all things" (Jacobs, *Hasidic Prayer* 21).

Yeshua taught that, because he is one with the Father and we are one with him, we are one with the Father (John 14:20). For Messianic believers—Jewish and Gentile—Yeshua transforms that ideal of oneness with God into reality.

Knowing God

Our goal is to "know" God. Bar Kappara stated that Proverbs 3:6 is a brief passage of Scripture upon which all the principles of *Torah* depend: "In all your ways acknowledge [know] him, and he will level your paths" (*Ber.* 63a). The *b'rakhot* are a form of prayer. They are central in the life of the religious Jewish person. Prayer is itself an indication of the desire to know God in all one's ways.

Sha'ul testified that he gave up everything of value in this life for the goal—"to know him" (Phil. 3:10). For *Sha'ul*, knowing Messiah meant entering into the "fellowship of his sufferings" and "the power of his resurrection." "Knowing," in this sense, is not cerebral. It is an intimate relationship, as between a husband and a wife.

Drawing Near

True prayer is surely a drawing near to God. Listen to Judah Halevi again:

> I have sought to come near to you,
> I have called to you with all my heart.
> (*Lord, Where Shall I Find You?*)

Hirsch encourages us "to strive through love to draw near to God" (359). He ties that drawing near with obedience to *Torah*. This is how we cling to God, how we know him—by walking in his ways.

Judaism teaches that this is the purpose of humanity's creation—to glorify God by the manner in which we live our lives. Luzzatto put it like this: "The chief function of man in this world is to keep the *mitzvot*, to worship God, and to withstand trial." He went on to say, "All man's strivings should be directed towards the Creator, blessed be he" (Leviant 559). Drawing near is more than *feeling*; it is *doing*. "The goal of all creation is the clinging of man to godliness" (Forst 26).

God promises to respond to us when we draw near. "Come to me," says Yeshua, ". . . and you will find rest for your souls" (Matt. 11:28–29). The tearing of the curtain before the Most Holy Place means, in one word, access. We may draw near, though not because we are acceptable in ourselves. Our Messiah opened the way when he gave his life for us.

Devekut and Holiness

Holiness is not an abstract idea. It is an objective practice "embodied in the concrete, the finite" (Sacks 273). We draw near as we recite the *b'rakhot.* In doing so, we should be devoting our whole lives to God. "All our acts can be imbued with holiness" (Forst 26). That is sanctification indeed. "Let all thy actions be for the Name of Heaven," said R. Jose (*Av.* 2:17). Nothing has any worth unless we do it to serve God. Believing in God, submitting to God, and practicing the *mitzvot* are inseparable. "If you love me," said Yeshua, "you will keep my commands" (John 14:15). It is as simple as that! "Faith by itself, unaccompanied by actions, is dead" (James 2:17).

The leaders of the Safed movement saw *devekut* differently. Their searching for God was a matter of great intensity. They felt they could only carry out this search in solitary contemplation. They practiced withdrawal, not only from society, but also from the body, seeking an ecstatic experience. This is not typical of Judaism, which sets a high value on the practice of the *mitzvot* in community. For the religious Jewish person, "eternity is not a refuge into which he wants to escape. It is something he wants to incorporate into the world" (Sacks 273). Yeshua taught the value of private prayer, but not as a purely subjective activity. Prayer is a means of making contact with God, so that he can have his way in our lives and in his world. God taking pleasure in me is far more important than me taking pleasure in God.

Devekut and Awe

Another aspect of *devekut* is awe of God. This awe should suffuse the whole of life. Ideally, there is never a moment when we are not conscious that God is in heaven and we are on earth. This is particularly true when we study the *Torah* or address God in prayer. "*B'rachos* [blessings] are inextricably tied to the awe and reverence that man is to experience in his relations to the Creator" (Forst 26). That is why we ought not to make a *b'rakhah* while doing something else. We should not interrupt a *b'rakhah*. Even our "amen" should be neither perfunctory nor hurried.

Yeshua, the Son of God, fell on his face when he prayed in Gethsemane. Nothing could be more indicative of respect—of awe. He had continuous, open access to *El Shaddai*. He had an intimate relationship with *Adonai Elohim*, addressing him as *Abba* (Dad). Yet, he bowed to the ground before the Father. Obedience flows from awe and respect, and so we hear him say, "Not what I want, but what you want" (Matt. 26:39).

Do we hold God in awe? Our attitude and obedient lives will reveal it.

Who Can Bless God?

You who live in the shelter of *'Elyon*,
who spend your nights in the shadow of *Shaddai*,
who say to ADONAI, "My refuge! My fortress!
My God, in whom I trust!" . . .

Because he loves me, I will rescue him;
because he knows my name, I will protect him.
He will call on me, and I will answer him.
I will be with him when he is in trouble.
I will extricate him and bring him honor.
I will satisfy him with long life
and show him my salvation. (Ps. 91:1–2, 14–16)

So, Let Us Bless the Lord!

Fount of my life! I bless thee while I live,
And sing my song to thee while being is mine!
    (Halevi, *Song of the Oppressed*)

My soul and my flesh wait for him and pant after him,
My Joy and my Portion, my Cup and my Maker,
Whom when I remember and mention, I feel
That nothing is more fitted for my soul's happiness
Than blessing the Name of the eternal God. (Gabirol, *Prayer*)

Bless ADONAI, my soul!
Everything in me, bless his holy Name! (Ps. 103:1–2)

Glossary

Adonai—Hebrew for "Lord." When in capital letters, it serves as a substitute for the ineffable Name of God, the Tetragrammaton.

Afikomen—Aramaic term used for the hidden portion of *matzah* eaten after the Passover meal.

Akiba ben Joseph—First-century C.E. rabbi. Known as "the father of rabbinical Judaism."

Alexanderer—Henoch. Nineteenth-century Hasidic rabbi.

Amidah—Hebrew for "standing." Refers to the "Standing Prayer," the eighteen blessings recited regularly in public and private worship. Also known as the *Shemoneh Esreh* (Eighteen Blessings).

B.C. and C.E.—Respectively, these terms stand for "before the common era" (a Jewish alternative to B.C.) and "common era" (a Jewish alternative to A.D.).

B'rakhah, b'rakhot (pl.)—Hebrew for "blessing." *B'rakhot* is also the name of the first tractate of the Talmud.

B'rit—Hebrew for "covenant."

B'rit Hadashah—Hebrew for "the New Testament."

Ba'al Shem Tov—Hebrew for "Master of the Good Name." Also known as the Besht (an acronym for "Baal Shem Tov"). Israel ben Eliezer, c.1700–1760, the founder of Hasidism.

Bar Kappara—Rabbi Eleazar HaKappar. Early third-century scholar and humanitarian.

Bar Kochba—Leader of the third and final Jewish revolt against Rome in the 130s C.E. Proclaimed messiah by Rabbi Akiba.

Barukh—Hebrew for "blessed." The name given to the first part of a *b'rakhah*.

Besht—See Baal Shem Tov.

Birkat haShir—Hebrew for "the Blessing of Song." A song of praise, traditionally ascribed by some to the apostle Peter.

Bratzlaver—Rabbi Nachman of Bratzlav, c.1772–1810. Great-grandson of the Besht. Considered by some to be greatest storyteller of the Jewish people.

Caro, Joseph—1488–1575, compiler of the *Shulchan Arukh,* the last great code of rabbinical Judaism.

Chillul haShem—Hebrew for "the Profanation of God's Name."

Devekut—Hebrew for "devotion." Refers to the right attitude in prayer.

Diaspora—The dispersion of Jewish people outside of Israel.

Eliezer of Worms—c.1165–1230, German Hasidic teacher.

Gamaliel, Rabban—Gamaliel II. Head of the Jewish community in Israel at the end of the first and the beginning of the second centuries C.E.

Gemara—Hebrew for "completion." Refers to the discussions on the *Mishnah.*

Great Synagogue—The body of elders who transmitted the traditions from the last of the biblical prophets to the earliest known scholars.

Haftarah—Hebrew for "conclusion." The portion from the Prophets, read immediately after the *Torah* reading in the morning services on Sabbaths, feast days, the ninth of Av, and in the afternoon services on fast days.

Hanukkah—Hebrew for "dedication." The festival commemorating the miracle of the multiplication of the oil, after the Maccabean victory in the second century B.C.E. It is celebrated by lighting candles or lamps on eight succeeding days by means of a "servant" light, until on the eighth day all eight are lit.

Hasid, Hasidim (pl.)—Hebrew for "pious one." Hasidism was founded in eighteenth-century Russia by the Baal Shem Tov. The Hasidic movement emphasizes Jewish mystical tradition, dynastic leadership (the *rebbe*), and joyful devotion to God through prayer, ecstatic worship, and study.

Hillel—A leading rabbi of the first century C.E. (see Shammai).

Judah Halevi—1085–1142, Spanish poet, philosopher, and physician.

Kaddish—Hebrew for "sanctification." Refers to the doxology recited, with congregational responses, at the close of prayers in the synagogue and after the burial service. It is a prayer that God's name be sanctified and magnified.

K'tuvim—The Writings; the third section of *Tanakh* (the Old Testament).

Kavanah—Hebrew for "intent, or "concentration. Refers to the attitude required for praying.

Kiddush haShem—Sanctification of the Name of God.

Kiddush—The blessing said before drinking wine.

Kobriner, Moses—Hasidic rabbi of the first half of the nineteenth century.

Kol Nidre—Hebrew for "All vows." The service held on the eve of *Yom Kippur*.

Lashon hara—Hebrew for "evil tongue." Negative comments or rumors.

Lipson, Eric—English Messianic Jew of the second half of the twentieth century.

Lulav—A palm branch used at the festival of *Sukkot*, together with myrtle and willow twigs, and a citron.

Luria, Isaac ben Solomon Ashkenazi—Sixteenth-century mystic, poet and teacher.

Luzzatto, Moses Hayim—1707–1747, philosopher and writer. Considered by some to be the founding father of modern Hebrew literature. Wrote *The Path of the Upright*, accepted as one of the finest works on practical ethics.

Maggid, Israel—The Maggid of Koznitz. Hasidic rabbi of the late eighteenth and early nineteenth centuries.

Maimonides—Moses ben Maimon. A twelfth-century talmudist, philosopher, astronomer, and physician. He formulated the Thirteen Principles of the Jewish Faith.

Malchut—Refers to the second part of the standard *b'rakhah*—*Melekh ha'olam* (King of the universe).

Mashiach—Hebrew for "Messiah, anointed."

Matzah—Hebrew for "unleavened bread." *Matzah* is eaten during Passover week to remember the haste with which the Jewish people had to leave Egypt (Exod. 12:14–20).

Meir—Rabbi, scholar, and teacher of the second century C.E.

Mishnah—Hebrew for "repetition." The code compiled by *Yehudah HaNasi*, c.200 C.E. The basis of Talmud.

Mitzvah, mitzvot (pl.)—Hebrew for "commandment" given by God. A good deed.

Moses Ibn Ezra—1055–1135. Spanish philosopher, linguist, and poet.

N'tilat Yadayim—The ritual washing of hands.

Nachmanides—Moses ben Nachman Gerondi, 1194–c.1270. Spanish talmudist, biblical scholar, and physician.

Nevi'im—The Prophets. The second part of *Tanakh.*

Omer—Hebrew for "sheaf." A sheaf of wheat or barley, symbolizing the counting of the fifty days between *Pesach* and *Shav'uot.*

Pesach—Passover. The festival commemorating the Exodus from Egypt.

Rashi—An acronym for Solomon bar Isaac, 1040–1105. French commentator on Bible and Talmud.

Rosh HaShanah—Hebrew for "Head of the Year." The traditional Jewish New Year, which is the beginning of a ten-day period of repentance leading up to *Yom Kippur.*

Ruach haKodesh—Hebrew for "the Holy Spirit."

Safed Movement—Sixteenth- and seventeenth-century rabbinic revival based at Safed, a small town in northern Galilee.

Sasson—Hebrew for "joy."

Seder—Hebrew for "order." Refers to the order of the ritual meal eaten at Passover to remember the Exodus from Egypt.

Selikhah—Hebrew for "repentance." *Selikhot* (pl.) are prayers of repentance.

Shabbat—Hebrew for "[day of] rest; Sabbath." *Shabbat* is the seventh day of the week (from Friday sunset to Saturday sunset). God commanded Israel to cease from work on this day and to assemble for worship (Exod. 20:8–11; Lev. 23:3).

Shaddai—Hebrew for "Almighty." *El Shaddai* (God Almighty) is one of the names of God.

Sha'ul—Paul

Sh'khinah—The glory of God, which went before the people as a cloud by day and fire by night. It came upon the Tabernacle at its completion and the Temple at its dedication. Said to be present with God's people when they pray and study *Torah.*

Sh'ma—Hebrew for "hear." The Jewish statement of faith: "Hear, O Israel! The Lord our God, the Lord is one. Blessed be his glorious Name, whose kingdom is forever and ever" (based on Deut. 6:4).

Shalom—Hebrew for "peace; wholeness."

Shammai—First-century C.E. scholar, a contemporary of Hillel. The Talmud records over three hundred differences of opinion between the schools of Hillel and Shammai.

Shavu'ot—The festival of Weeks; Pentecost.

Shehekhiyanu—Refers to the *b'rakhah* that blesses God for keeping us alive, sustaining us, and bringing us to this season.

Shem (HaShem)—Hebrew for "name." The Name of God. A synonym for God himself.

Shemoneh Esreh—The eighteen blessings of the *Amidah*.

Siddur—Hebrew for prayer book.

Simeon ben Lakish—Third-century C.E. scholar.

Simeon ben Yochai—Second-century C.E. Kabbalist. Said to have compiled the Zohar. Kabbalism is an esoteric branch of Judaism.

Simchah—Hebrew for "joy."

Simchat Torah—The "Rejoicing over the Law." The festival at the end of *Sukkot*.

Solomon Ibn Gabirol—c.1021–1058. Spanish poet, philosopher, moralist.

Sukkah, sukkot (pl.)—Hebrew for "booth." A temporary shelter made of wood and foliage. Jews are commanded to dwell in a *sukkah* during the feast of *Sukkot* (Lev. 23:42).

Sukkot—The Feast of Booths, or Tabernacles, commemorating Israel's forty years in the desert before entering the Promised Land. During this period, Israel was vulnerable to the elements and fully dependent on God, a reality symbolized by their dwelling in *sukkot* (Lev. 23:33–43; Deut. 8).

Talmid, talmidim (pl.)—Hebrew for disciple, disciples.

Teshuvah—Hebrew for "turning" or "repentance."

Talmud—Complex anthology of Jewish law and the traditions that accumulated around that law, regarded as authoritative in Judaism.

Tanakh—Hebrew acronym from the words *Torah* (Teaching), *Nevi'im* (Prophets), and *K'tuvim* (Writings); i.e., the Hebrew Scriptures (see Luke 24:44).

Tefillah—Hebrew for "prayer."

Tefillin—Hebrew for "prayers." Also, Small leather boxes containing Scripture on parchments that are bound to the forehead and upper right arm of a Jew during morning prayers (except on *Shabbat* and festivals). The purpose of *tefillin* is devotional (Deut. 6:8).

Tehillim—Psalms.

Tetragrammaton—The ineffable Name of God, composed of four letters—יהוה (YHWH).

Torah—Hebrew for "Teaching." Torah refers to the five books of Moses; the Law or Teaching of God.

Tosefta—Hebrew for "additions; extensions." The collection of later comments on Talmud.

Tzedakah—Hebrew for "righteousness" or "charity."

Tzva'ot—Hebrew for "armies." ADONAI *Tzva'ot* is one of the names of God.

Tzaddik—Hebrew for "a righteous man."

Yehudah HaNasi—Rabbi, c.135–c.220. Redactor of the Mishnah.

Yeshua—Hebrew for "*Adonai* [the Lord] saves." Yeshua is Jesus' Hebrew name.

Yom Kippur—Hebrew for "Day of Atonement." The holiest day of the Jewish calendar; a fast day, the culmination of a ten-day period of repentance and prayer for the forgiveness of sin (Lev. 16; 23:26–32).

Yom Tov—Hebrew for "a good day." Refers to any festival day.

Yomtov of York—Leader of the York (England) Jewish community at the time of the Massacre of York in 1190. The Jewish community, taking shelter in York Castle, were offered the alternatives of baptism or death. They committed mass suicide.

Bibliography

Adler, S. Alfred. "The Mystery of Pain." *A Book of Jewish Thoughts.* Comp. J. H. Hertz, 296–297. Oxford: Oxford UP, 1920.

Authorised Daily Prayer Book (ADP). Trans. Rev. S. Singer. London: Eyre & Spottiswoode, 1957.

"Benedictions." *The Jewish Encyclopedia.* Ed. Isidore Singer. New York and London: Funk & Wagnalls, 1901, 3:8–13.

Budoff, Barry A. *A Messianic Jewish Siddur for Shabbat.* N.p. July 23,1999.

Cohen, Abraham. *Everyman's Talmud.* London: Dent & Sons, 1932.

Domnitz, Myer. *Judaism.* London: Ward Lock Educational, 1970.

Donin, Hayim Halevy. *To Pray as a Jew.* New York: Basic, 1980.

Epstein, Isidore. *Step by Step in the Jewish Religion.* London: Soncino, 1958.

Fiddler on the Roof. Dir. Norman Jewison. Mirisch, 1971.

Fine, Lawrence. "The Contemplative Practice of Yihudim in Lurianic Kabbalah." *Jewish Spirituality from the Sixteenth-Century Revival to the Present.* Ed. Arthur Green, 64–98. London: SCM, 1988.

Forst, Binyamin. *The Laws of B'rachos.* New York: Mesorah, 1990.

Friedlander, M. *The Jewish Religion.* London: Shapiro, Vallentine, 1922.

Gabirol, Solomon Ibn. "Prayer." *Masterpieces of Hebrew Literature.* Ed. Curt Leviant, 181. New York: KTAV, 1969.

Ginsburgh, Yitzchak. *The Alef-Beit.* Northvale: Aronson, 1995.

Green, A. A. "Resignation." *A Book of Jewish Thoughts.* Comp. J. H. Hertz, 315. Oxford: Oxford UP, 1920.

Halevi, Judah. "For the Day of Atonement." *The Penguin Book of Hebrew Verse.* Ed and Trans. T. Carmi, 336. Middlesex: Penguin, 1981.

———. "Lord, Where Shall I Find You?" *The Penguin Book of Hebrew Verse.* Ed and Trans. T. Carmi, 338–339. Middlesex: Penguin, 1981.

———. "My Heart Is in the East." *The Penguin Book of Hebrew Verse.* Ed and Trans. T. Carmi, 347. Middlesex: Penguin, 1981.

———. "Song of the Oppressed." *Masterpieces of Hebrew Literature.* Ed. Curt Leviant, 200. New York: KTAV, 1969.

————. "The Home of Love." *The Penguin Book of Hebrew Verse.* Ed and Trans. T. Carmi, 333–334. Middlesex: Penguin, 1981.

Hertz, J. H. *A Book of Jewish Thoughts.* Oxford: Oxford UP, 1920.

————. *The Authorised Daily Prayer Book with Commentary.* London: National Council for Jewish Education, 1943.

————. *The Pentateuch and Haftorahs—Leviticus.* Oxford: Oxford UP, 1932.

Hirsch, Samson Raphael. *Horeb.* Trans. I. Grunfeld. London: Soncino, 1962.

Holy Bible: New International Version. London, Sydney, Auckland: Hodder & Stoughton, 1973.

Holy Bible: New Revised Standard Version. New York, Oxford: Oxford UP, 1989.

Jacobs, Louis. *Hasidic Prayer.* New York: Schocken, 1973.

————. *Principles of the Jewish Faith.* London: Vallentine, Mitchell, 1964.

————. *Theology in the Responsa.* London: Routledge & Kegan Paul, 1975.

Kidner, Derek. *A Commentary on the Psalms.* London: InterVarsity Press, 1975.

Klausner, Joseph. *The Messianic Idea in Israel.* London: Allen & Unwin, 1956.

Lapide, Pinchas. *The Resurrection of Jesus.* London: SPCK, 1983.

Leivick, H. "The Night Is Dark." In *Siddur Lev Chadash.* Ed. Rabbi John D. Raynor and Rabbi Chaim Stern, 289. London: Union of Liberal and Progressive Synagogues, 1995. Originally published in *The Penguin Book of Yiddish Verse.* Ed. Irving Howe, Ruth R. Wisse, and Khone Shmeruk. London: Penguin, 1987.

Luzzatto, Moses Hayim. "The Path of the Upright." *Masterpieces of Hebrew Literature.* Ed. Curt Leviant, 551–569. New York: KTAV, 1969.

Montefiore, C. G. and H. Loewe. *A Rabbinic Anthology.* London: Macmillan, 1938.

Newman, Louis I. *The Hasidic Anthology.* New York and London: Scribner's Sons, 1934.

Ross, Lesli Koppelman. *Celebrate.* Northvale: Aronson, 1994.

Rossel, Seymour. *When a Jew Prays.* New York: Behrman, 1973.

Sacks, Jonathan. "Credo." *The Times* (London). 22 February 2003, 46.

————. "Message for Rosh HaShanah." Television broadcast. England, 1999.

————. *Tradition in an Untraditional Age.* London: Vallentine, Mitchell, 1990.

Siddur Lev Chadash. Ed. Rabbi John D. Raynor and Rabbi Chaim Stern. London: Union of Liberal and Progressive Synagogues, 1995.

Steinsaltz, Adin. *The Talmud, A Reference Guide.* New York: Random House, 1989.

Telushkin, Joseph. *Jewish Wisdom.* New York: Morrow, 1994.

The Encyclopedia of Judaism. Judaic Classics Library. CD-ROM. Jerusalem: Davka, 1989.

The Soncino Talmud. Judaic Classics Library. CD-ROM. New York: Davka, 1991-95.